HEAVENLY HUMOR
for the
Teacher's Soul

HEAVENLY HUMOR

for the

Teacher's Soul

75 Inspirational Readings
(with Class!)

BARBOUR
PUBLISHING

CONTENTS

Section 1—New Teacher's Survival Guide: Strength

Rotten Eggs 11
The Day of Evelyn's Faint. 13
Run with Me 16
The Rest of the Story 18
Keeping Cool in a Hot Flash 21
Teepee or Not to Teepee. 24
Do As I Say 26
Waiting for Shekinah Glory. 28

Section 2—First Daze: Wisdom

The Midnight Ride of Paul Revere 33
Lip Service. 36
Naomi's Big Payoff. 39
The Lost Tooth Club 41
Best-Laid Plans of Mice and Teachers. 43
Warning: Dangerous Contents. 46
New Clothes 49
Resisting the *Eeww!* 51

Section 3—Tales from the Teacher's Lounge: Humor

Holiday Library Humor. 57
Mr. Cutler, My Fifth-Grade Jokester Teacher 59
Finger Work. 61
Always Ready. 63
Laugh It Up! 66

Section 4—Confessions of a Substitute: Trust

Getting to the Bottom of Things 71

Holding 73

Chinchilla Consequence 75

There's Always Homework 77

Stressed Out! 79

Substitute Teaching and Sinking Ships 81

Section 5—A Teacher's Homework: Love

Gathering Bits of Fuzz 87

Plenty of the Good Stuff 89

Boy Crazy 92

Pink Whirling Confection 94

King Tut 96

People Watchers 98

Someone to Watch Over Me 101

Cheerleaders and Wiener Dogs 104

Pink Cadillacs and Encouraging Words 106

Teacher's Pet 108

Be a Giver 110

Fitting In 112

Communication Gap 114

Section 6—Not Another Apple: Patience

Feather Girl 119

The Long Way Home 122

Going to See the Rabbits 124

Not Exactly As It Appears 127

Bad Day. 129
No Talking. 131

Section 7—Teaching Outside the Box: Dedication
Copilots. 137
What If I Have No Talent?. 140
Got the Goods. 142
Learn Your Lesson Well 144
Pet Peeves and Teacher's Mugs 146
Snakes Alive! 148

Section 8—The Teacher as Student: Forgiveness
When I Say, "Quiet. . ." 153
Scrap Distraction 156
Hoping Hard. 158
Starting at the Beginning 160
What the Student Taught the Teacher 162
Prank Night. 165
Bangles and Boldness. 167

Section 9—Testing, Testing: Discipline
The Hard Line 171
Heart Dissection 174
Break a Leg 176
A Skunk in the Trunk 178
Thanks for Flunking Me 180
High as a Kite 182
Running in Circles. 185

Section 10—God's Lesson Plans: Obedience

Color-Coding the Library 191

Dad's Wisdom as a Teacher 194

Name Game. 196

Let Your Light Shine 199

All or Nothing 201

Beginning at the End. 204

Ice Cream Zoo. 206

Soccer. . .Broadway Style 209

To Give or Not to Give 211

New Teacher's Survival Guide: Strength

By learning you will teach;
by teaching you will understand.

LATIN PROVERB

ROTTEN EGGS

Jean Fischer

"Watch and pray so that you will not fall into temptation.
The spirit is willing, but the flesh is weak."
MARK 14:38 NIV

Years ago, when I was a college student, I spent a summer as a teacher's aide. In the remedial kindergarten class I was assigned to, the teacher spent most of her time reviewing up, down, inside, outside, and how to bounce a ball. The kids and I were bored silly. We all let out a sigh of relief when she announced that the following week we'd be taking some field trips.

Whoever planned these trips had to be out of his or her mind: the plans included a jaunt to a monastery to see Brother Anthony's bee hives, an excursion to a theater group's rehearsal of *Hamlet*, and a trip to a duck-egg farm.

When we arrived at the monastery, Brother Anthony met us wearing white coveralls and a beekeeper's hat and veil. He offered a long and complex explanation of the fine points of beekeeping. Then he led us to the hives. The sight of bees buzzing around the tall, white boxes sent half the class running back to the bus. The other kids swatted the bees, against the advice of Brother Anthony, and ten minutes and two bee stings later, we were on our way back to school.

The next morning, bright and early, we all held hands and walked a mile to the community theater. *To be or not to be,* that was the question. A scary ghost and dialogue way beyond a five-year-old's comprehension convinced the kids not to be, and before long, we were back in class practicing inside, outside, up, and down.

I looked forward to the last field trip. How bad could the egg farm be? A ride in the country on a hot summer day, cute little duckies, and maybe even scrambled eggs as a treat?

We arrived in the bus with the windows open.

"Ooo, it stinks!" said little Kevin. "Do ducks smell or did somebody go to the bathroom?"

Leave it to Kevin to explore all the possibilities. But he was right, the egg farm stank.

We held our noses as a guide led us past dozens of white ducks sitting on their nests and then inside a building where workers at a conveyer belt inspected eggs and cast off imperfect ones.

"What's this?" Kevin exclaimed. He ran to a tall round vat near the end of the conveyer belt. Before I could grab him, Kevin scrambled up, peeked inside, and fell head first into the heap of discarded rotten eggs! He stank so bad on the ride home that several students threw up.

As Christians we all face temptation. None of us are perfect. But when curiosity beckons us to "look inside" and we fall into that stinking bin of rotten eggs, God provides us a way out—Jesus Christ. We can be grateful that He died in our place so our sins will be forgiven.

THE DAY OF EVELYN'S FAINT

Kathy Douglas

If any of you lacks wisdom, you should ask God, who gives generously to all without finding fault, and it will be given to you.

JAMES 1:5 NIV

Mr. Tovey's teaching career began and ended my sixth-grade year. I have a picture of Mr. Tovey in an old photo album. Like many field trips back in those days, teachers and parents drove kids to special outings. None of this big yellow school bus stuff with signed consents. We all piled into the cars of a variety of volunteers and off we went.

In that grainy photo, Mr. Tovey is driving his Volkswagen "Bug" packed with sixth-grade boys. One of them is half standing with his head sticking up through the opened Volkswagen roof. Mr. Tovey has an affable grin on his face. He's ready to enjoy this outing even though one guy in his Volkswagen looks like a giraffe in a pony cage.

I have another image of Mr. Tovey from that year that didn't make it into any photo album: the day of Evelyn's faint.

Back in December of my sixth-grade year, months before that spring field trip, our class practiced for a Christmas program in the school auditorium. As we stood on rickety wooden risers, Mr. Tovey directed our singing. Suddenly, our classmate, Evelyn—known to everyone except our inexperienced teacher as a regular "fainter"—slipped from sight.

With no drama or panic, one of the kids said, "Mr. Tovey, Evelyn just fainted." As in, "Yeah, she's down again. No big deal."

For poor Mr. Tovey, it was quite a big deal.

With no cell phones, no school nurse, and no 911 then, he ran for help. Moments later he came running back with a woman from the office who was not running, but yawning. Mr. Tovey's black hair and horn-rimmed glasses contrasted starkly with his colorless, sweat-drenched face. Evelyn herself had already rallied and stood ready to sing again.

The office secretary mumbled something like, "You see? She's fine," and promptly left the auditorium and our ghostly Mr. Tovey behind.

Like Mr. Tovey, several of the Lord's disciples came up against something they, too, had not bargained for during their training. A boy thrashed around with a seizure because of demon oppression. With raw desperation, the father said to Jesus, "I brought [my son] to your disciples, but they could not heal him" (Matthew 17:16 NIV).

Imagine the hapless, speechless disciples thinking, "Hey, we didn't sign up for *this*!"

Just as they did for the disciples, things come to us as teachers for which we have little or no training. On days like that, we want to run out of the room and find a less intimidating job—like getting shot out of a cannon. Or maybe exorcising a demon.

Just as Jesus healed the boy and used the occasion to teach His men about faith, He can help us in our difficult, unplanned circumstances, too.

Jesus' disciples lived to "do even greater things" (see John 14:12). Mr. Tovey, however, didn't return to our school the next year. The day of Evelyn's faint had done him in.

RUN WITH ME

Shelley R. Lee

There is surely a future hope for you, and your hope will not be cut off.
Listen, my son, and be wise, and keep your heart on the right path.
PROVERBS 23:18–19 NIV

The first-grade class was running laps around the basketball court to get warmed up before gym class.

Several children grumbled, "How much longer?" as they huffed and puffed their way slowly past me.

Jacob ran past me on his quick little legs. "Can we keep going?" he managed to ask between breaths.

"No, there's a toll booth!" one of Jacob's classmates answered, attempting to use his imagination to assist his fatigue.

Later in the class, little Claire didn't want to play capture the flag. She couldn't quite understand the rules, and the children who were much stronger and confident were running circles around the "Claires" of the class. The whole ordeal seemed just too overwhelming for her. Then, just when it seemed hopeless, her smiling friend came alongside her and grabbed her hand. Claire lit up like Christmas morning, and her whole attitude changed in an instant.

The two little girls headed joyfully, hand in hand, skipping in sync toward the other side of the gym. Neither was concerned about winning the game, but they were immensely happy.

As I observed that sweet gesture and the incredible difference it made for Claire, I realized there have been countless times when God gave me just the encouragement I needed to get back in the game. Sometimes it was a friend who stopped by just in time, sometimes a good word from a book, or a song. Other times creation has shown me a bit of God's glory, so I don't lose hope. God is infinitely creative in the ways He sends encouragement when I need it.

Furthermore, He knows that I need to enjoy my place in the game, no matter what it is, more than I need to win the game.

God knows that sometimes I just need someone to slip a hand in mine and run along with me.

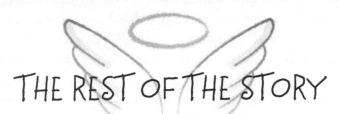

THE REST OF THE STORY

Roberta Tucker Brosius

Read these laws and teachings to the people. . . . And each new generation
will listen and learn to worship the Lord their God with fear and
trembling and to do exactly what is said in God's Law.
DEUTERONOMY 31:11–13 CEV

M r. Roberts decided it was time for me to teach a Bible story.
I hadn't grown up in a Christian home or attended Sunday
school, but I became a Christian at age twelve. A few years later, as a
teenage member of a ministry team, I spent Sunday afternoons visiting
inner-city housing projects to hold outdoor meetings for children.
After learning to lead the kids in singing action songs like, "I'm in
the Lord's Army," and, "Deep and Wide," I progressed to introducing
Bible verses using a hangman-style game, filling in the letters as the
kids guessed them.

But now Mr. Roberts, my spiritual father and mentor, decided it
was time for me to teach the Bible story on a Sunday in the near future.
He bought several flannel-graph packets, and I chose the story of Jonah
the Prophet and took it home to prepare.

Having never seen a flannel-graph lesson before—the other team members hadn't used them—I had no idea that the fuzzy-backed Bible people would magically stick to a board covered with flannel. So I came up with my own method: I searched the house for construction paper and glue. As always, it took hot water, a straight pin, and several minutes to unclog the pull-up cap of the Elmer's glue bottle. I carefully punched out the perforated people. . .and used Scotch tape to repair the ones I dismembered. It's a good thing the packet provided several versions of Jonah, the sailors, the Ninevites, and the big fish, or the tale would have ended after showing one picture. With the multiple figures provided, I created a picture for each scene in the story, putting story notes on the back of each paper in case I forgot.

As I prepared the lesson, I became indignant—what a terrible ending! Jonah went off and pouted because he didn't get his own way. I couldn't tell that to young children.

Several weeks later our team climbed into Mr. Roberts's old Plymouth and traveled to Paterson, New Jersey. It was finally time to teach my first Bible story, and except for the butterflies bumping off my stomach walls, I was ready. Following the songs and the Bible verse puzzle, I stood in front of the children.

Holding up my carefully crafted pictures one by one, I told them about Jonah's adventure. However, I ended the story right after the people of Nineveh repented—omitting Jonah's reaction—thus giving me and my listeners a happily ever after conclusion.

Mr. Roberts never commented on the messed up flannel graph, or the abridged Bible story, but continued to encourage my growth as a Christian and development as a teacher.

I have taught hundreds of Bible lessons to people of all ages in the forty-plus years since. Along the way, I came to understand that I have to share all of God's Word with my students, not just selections that are happy and easy to understand.

And I finally figured out how to use those fuzzy flannel graphs.

KEEPING COOL IN A HOT FLASH

Janice Hanna

*For the trumpet will sound, the dead will be
raised imperishable, and we will be changed.*
I CORINTHIANS 15:52 NIV

Menopause is nothing to laugh about. Well, maybe it is, but I've never found it terribly funny. . .until one night a few years ago when I'd been called upon to teach at a writing group in another city. As a newly published author, I longed to teach the writing craft to others.

Arriving early, I set up my book table and prepared to teach. The evening began on a good note. I managed to share helpful writing tidbits for several minutes, keeping my nerves under control. Then, just about the time I thought everything was running smoothly, the strangest thing happened. My face suddenly felt like it was on fire. I could feel the heat rising, and for a moment, thought I might pass out. *Ugh!* I tried to keep talking, but my mind went blank. I had this weird out-of-body experience and wondered if I'd be able to keep going. From across the room, I caught the eye of my friend Sharen, who'd come along to support me. Her eyes were wide. Clearly, she knew I was in trouble.

I somehow got things under control, and the heat wave eventually passed. I calmed down and continued my teaching. Afterward, I made my apologies to the director of the writing group and went in search of my friend. She couldn't help but laugh as we talked through what had happened.

"Your face was bright red!" she said.

"No doubt. It felt like someone lit a fire inside of me."

"How old are you again?" she whispered.

"Forty-five."

"Mm-hmm." She crossed her arms at her chest and nodded. "I figured it must be that. In fact, I was sure of it."

"That. . .what?"

"You were having a hot flash, honey! You're starting to go through 'the change'!"

No way. I couldn't believe it. Who else had their very first hot flash in front of a roomful of students? And what did she mean. . .the change? Did I really need to change? If so, did it have to happen in front of so many strangers, and in such a public way?

I still remember the embarrassment of that night—the confusion of not knowing what was happening, the awkwardness of thinking I might faint in front of a roomful of strangers, the apologies I issued after the fact. Worst of all, I felt like I'd let the group's director down.

What has stood out to me, however, is that phrase, "going through the change." As I ponder it now, I realize that sometimes God has to light a fire under us to get the sort of change He's looking for in our lives. Oh, I'm not talking hot flashes. (I would never say those are from God!) I'm just convinced that He's ready to heat things up a bit to mold us into His image.

These days, I have a lot of "flashes" that leave me in a sweat. Like millions of other women, I do my best to muddle through them. But I'm constantly reminded that, as I'm going through physical changes in my life, God longs to change my heart as well. Hopefully He won't have to resort to fire to accomplish it.

TEEPEE OR NOT TO TEEPEE

Connie L. Peters

*"If your brother or sister sins, go and point out their fault, just between
the two of you. If they listen to you, you have won them over."*
MATTHEW 18:15 NIV

At thirty-one, Nancy went into her first teaching assignment,
confident she'd be able to handle teaching English to high school
seniors. She didn't realize what battle lay before her, when some
determined students conspired against her.

One autumn morning, her yard looked like a winter wonderland
with what must have been several economy packs of toilet paper strung
through her trees, bushes, and over her house. If only the vandals
would be as thorough and creative with their assignments as they were
with decorating her yard!

The next day, she said not a word but gave a pop quiz to all her
classes. Several incidents of teepee-ing after that, she said nothing but
gave the traditional after-teepee pop quiz. She figured eventually the
innocent kids would flush the rascals out. Her break came not from
irritated classmates, but her youngest on tiptoe on the couch looking
out the window exclaiming, "Ooooh, pretty!"

Nancy dashed to the window. "Aha!" She caught the delinquent landscape artists in action! She raced out to their truck, grabbed the keys, and ran back into the house with a firm slam of the door. She clutched the keys to herself and smiled. The truck owner, Todd, and his five accomplices grabbed what was left of their arsenal, managed to start the keyless truck, and drove off.

Now she knew her opponents but still said nothing to anyone, though Todd was the son of one of her fellow teachers. There were a lot of things a teacher could get into trouble for; she felt it was worth taking a risk. She kept it between herself and Todd. Though he seemed to get along without his truck key, she still had his house key and his mother's car key. And every day she'd have another student drive Todd's truck to a different spot in the parking lot, forcing him to search for his vehicle.

Finally, Todd approached her. "Let's call a truce," he said.

"I'll give your keys back," she bargained, "if you patrol my house on Halloween." It turned out to be a good deal for both teacher and student. Now, thirty years later, Todd still keeps in touch with Nancy and has always appreciated that she didn't snitch but outwitted him. And it gives Nancy satisfaction to think of Todd getting his just desserts by having kids of his own.

The Bible says when disagreements happen we're to first try to work things out among ourselves. God's goal is always a mended, whole relationship. Nancy saw her students as more valuable than her yard, her time, and even her desire for justice. Likewise, God's goal is to bring us into close relationship with Him, even when we misuse our resources.

DO AS I SAY

Darlene Franklin

*In everything set them an example by doing what is good.
In your teaching show integrity, seriousness and soundness
of speech that cannot be condemned.*

TITUS 2:7–8 NIV

My age: fifteen. My enthusiasm: 1,000 percent. My training: completed, as much as a few weeks attending teacher training classes would allow. My role model: my mother.

My assignment: to teach the beginners' Sunday school class in our tiny church. My poor pastor. His two oldest children were the only regular attendees in the class, and for their teacher, they had me, a teenager only ten years older than they were. My mother taught the primary grades. I had enjoyed Mrs. Bailey's junior class, but I yawned my way through youth Sunday school.

As one of the few to complete the teacher training offered at church, I was invited to teach preschoolers during their crucial, formative years. I don't recall what the teacher training included; nor could I tell you what kind of lesson plans the teacher's guide suggested. I do remember the clean (read: bare) walls, the low-lying table that ran the length of one wall, the child-sized chairs. Our newly built, sparsely furnished space lacked the different learning centers that later came to dominate preschool classrooms. Whatever we did (all three of us, after all), we did together. We had a story time, some kind of art activity, and occasionally something special.

For one story—Jesus at the Mount of Olives? A story including olive oil? I confess I don't remember—I came up with the bright idea of letting my students taste olives. Even back then I knew that taste and smell, as well as sight, hearing, and touch, aided the learning process.

Since I didn't eat olives myself, I didn't realize there were different kinds of olives. Without access to the Internet which I now take for granted, I didn't even consider researching olive production in Jesus' time. I brought a jar of olives—green, with red pimento centers—for my two students to try.

I was quite proud of myself for the idea. This would be a memorable lesson, I thought. Better than scratching crayons over and through the black lines of a coloring picture.

The lesson proved memorable, all right. At the appropriate time, I opened the jar of olives and offered them to little Anita and Lauren. Surprise, surprise. They didn't take the bait.

"Just try it." My brain scrambled for a solution and came up with the obvious answer. I must try one myself. I plucked an olive out of the jar using a tiny fork and popped it in my mouth.

I refrained from spitting it back out—just barely. But my face said it all. Needless to say, neither child *ever* ate an olive on that morning. My example accomplished the opposite of its desired effect.

A teacher's example in the classroom will impact her students more than any words she might say. Whether I'm drawing stick figures, or correcting a wayward pupil. . .or eating olives. . .I want them to see past my mistakes. I want them to see Christ in me.

WAITING FOR SHEKINAH GLORY

Gena Maselli

This is love: not that we loved God, but that he loved us and sent his Son as an atoning sacrifice for our sins.
1 JOHN 4:10 NIV

I'm having trouble," I said. "Elliana doesn't want to do school. What am I doing wrong?"

My friend Camille was an experienced homeschool mom with five children, whose ages ranged from a toddler taking his first steps to a high school senior on the cusp of graduation. She had seen it all. Her home always seemed to be peaceful. . .quite different from mine lately.

As a new homeschooling mother, my approach to educating my children was on par with an army general about to capture his first stronghold. I had read the recommended books, gleaned information from more experienced teachers, and stocked my home with the best curriculum.

I was convinced that I could give my child a quality education that moved at her own pace and inspired her to fall in love with learning.

I had been swept away by the promise of a glorious educational experience, one in which she floated to our table with a twinkle in her eye and a thirst for knowledge. I wanted no less than a divine experience—with the Shekinah Glory raining down from heaven.

Instead, I got a roll of the eyes and a shrug of the shoulders. "Do we *have* to do school today?"

I shared my frustrations with my friend. "So at what point do we see the Shekinah Glory?"

My friend laughed.

She then began to teach me about real, nitty-gritty homeschooling. "You do what you have to do to teach them," she said. "Sometimes that means saying, 'You are going to sit in that chair until this is done.' Sometimes it means finding a fresh way to teach the material."

She shared how she had, at times, put the books away to get on her children's levels. She admitted to using *Star Wars* action figures to teach her son math. *If Chewbacca removes one arm from a storm trooper, how many appendages does the storm trooper have left?* Then she talked about defining education as more than merely academics, but also character and godliness.

I listened with rapt attention, gleaning all I could from her wisdom. Her message gave me ideas for ways to improve my own techniques and engage my daughter by teaching on her level.

The idea of getting on a child's level gave me pause. God did the same with me, hadn't He? When He sent His Son Jesus to pay the price for my—and everyone else's—sin, He got down from His throne and taught us in a way we could understand. He opened our minds and our hearts to His grace and love.

I went home with a renewed purpose for teaching my daughter

and a greater appreciation for what God did through His Son. Thank God He loved us enough to lift us out of our sin so we could communicate with Him. Sometimes the greatest lessons are those that come while we wait for the Shekinah Glory. . .lessons that remind us of what we already know.

First Daze:
Wisdom

To learn and never be filled, is wisdom;
to teach and never be weary, is love.

UNKNOWN

THE MIDNIGHT RIDE OF PAUL REVERE

Jean Fischer

*We should be grateful that we were given a kingdom that
cannot be shaken. And in this kingdom we please God by
worshiping him and by showing him great honor and respect.*
HEBREWS 12:28 CEV

In 1 Samuel 8, we read that the people of Israel decided not to put all their trust in the Lord. Instead, they asked for a king. This upset Samuel, so he took it to the Lord, and the Lord said, "Do everything they ask, but warn them and tell them how a king will treat them" (verse 9 CEV).

I thought of this Old Testament story when I taught my students about the American Revolution. Britain's King George had much in common with the king that Samuel warned his people about. He lived an affluent lifestyle and lorded over his subjects. He imposed heavy taxes on the people, and he made them suffer as a result of his rules.

I explained the rules of King George to my class and also about how the American colonists decided to fight against them. Then we discussed the midnight ride of Paul Revere.

"British soldiers, called *redcoats*, were on their way to Lexington, Massachusetts," I explained. "A man named Paul Revere was an express rider, and it was his job to warn the people that the soldiers might attack. The story goes that Paul Revere rode all night warning people along the way that enemy soldiers were coming. He shouted to everyone, 'The redcoats are coming! The redcoats are coming!' "

The next day, I asked the class to review what they had learned about Paul Revere and his midnight ride.

A blond-haired boy, sitting in the last row of desks, raised his hand. I was thrilled, because Tristan often seemed preoccupied and didn't pay attention in class.

"Yes, Tristan!" I said. "What did you learn about Paul Revere?"

"Well," he began. "There was this mean guy, a king named *Britain* that nobody liked, and our guys were fighting with him. So, Paul Revere rode through town hollering, 'The yellow jackets are coming!' to warn everybody that the bad guys were on the way."

Impressed that he'd gotten most of the story right, I asked for more.

"Are you sure the king's soldiers were called *yellow jackets*?" I prodded.

After thinking for a few seconds, Tristan answered, "Yes."

"Why?" I asked, allowing him one more chance to get the answer right.

"Because," he explained confidently, "yellow jackets are bees, and bees attack and they sting you. That's why King Britain called his soldiers the yellow jackets!"

History was rewritten in my classroom that day.

We serve the Lord our God, the mightiest of kings. We needn't worry about Him enslaving us and imposing rules designed to hurt us. Whenever we disagree with our leaders, the most important thing is to place our trust in God and remember, "The LORD is King for ever and ever." (Psalm 10:16 NIV).

LIP SERVICE

Kathy Douglas

Jesus replied. . ."Isaiah was right when he prophesied about you,
for he wrote, 'These people honor me with their lips,
but their hearts are far from me.' "

MARK 7:6–7 NLT

Christy found herself at the end of the indignant teacher's wagging finger.

"*Villiam's* English is terrible! Practice! He must practice his English!"

Christy was shocked. Like her other two children, William attended a Russian school in Moscow where their family lives. Classes in English are required for all students in Russia, even if they're Americans. Since William's first language was English, his mother couldn't understand why his Russian English teacher criticized William's spoken English.

What could be the problem?

Christy knows William's command of English grammar's finer points isn't much better than any American boy his age, but *spoken* English? Her son's exceptional bilingualism amazed her, her husband, and the Russians they come in contact with. Whenever they met Russians for the first time, they all thought William was Russian.

"He's an American? He talks like a Russian!" people would say, or "Your son's Russian is flawless!" "His Russian is too good. He *must* be Russian."

None of his American friends or family have ever noticed a problem with William's English either. So why this trouble with English all of a sudden?

Christy decided some detective work was in order. She stood outside her youngest son's classroom during English recitation. The teacher held up a series of pictures, and the class recited after her.

Teacher: "*Dis* is cat."

Class: "*Dis* is cat."

Teacher: "*Dis* is dog."

Class: "*Dis* is dog."

Teacher: "*Dis* is pig."

The only exception in the harmonious responses was a slumping, bored William, who said loudly, "*This* is cat. . . . *This* is dog. . . . *This* is. . ."

"William," Christy said to her son that evening, "when you do recitation in English class, repeat what the teacher says exactly."

"But Mom. . ."

"I know. But very few Russians can pronounce the 'th' sound. Just do as she does."

"But it's *wrong*! She's not saying it right! None of them are!"

"I know, William, but just do as she does."

The next day in English class, William mimicked what he heard.

"Dis is cat."

The teacher beamed as everyone in her class repeated her sounds exactly—including the American student. William slouched in his chair doing what he was told, but not liking it.

Do I obey God like William obeyed Christy? Do I do what I should do or have to do or ought to do with a slovenly attitude or a heart of rebellion?

Do "the will of God from your heart" reads Ephesians 6:6 (NIV). I want to obey God and do His will wholeheartedly. Mere lip service may be enough in a Russian classroom, but Jesus knows the attitudes I harbor behind all my words. Unlike an obedient but obstinate William slouching at his desk, I want my words and actions to spring from an obedient heart.

The next time Christy saw William's teacher, she wagged no pointing finger.

"*Villiam* is doing much better in English." She beamed with the pride of accomplishment. "*Dis* is *vonderful* improvement!"

William rolled his eyes, but Christy only smiled.

NAOMI'S BIG PAYOFF

Roberta Tucker Brosius

They received the message with great eagerness and examined the Scriptures every day to see if what Paul said was true.

ACTS 17:11 NIV

While repeating the question, I surveyed my sixth-period high school Bible students. Bored. Barely awake. Slouched in their seats. Slumped over their open Bibles and notebooks. The last academic class of the day was a killer. It didn't matter how exciting the subject matter was, the students wanted the bell to ring.

But the book of Acts excites me, and particularly chapter 12 where the prayers of Peter's friends resulted in an angel releasing him from prison. King Herod Agrippa the First had already executed James, the son of Zebedee, and intended to do the same to Peter.

So I asked yet again, "When did Herod plan to execute Peter?" I waited impatiently for someone—anyone—to respond, "After Passover."

Only Naomi spoke, and I pretended not to hear her ridiculous answer, "After Easter."

I kept asking the same question, and Naomi kept answering "Easter." Exasperated, I exclaimed, "Naomi, if you can show me the word *Easter* in the Bible, I'll give you a thousand dollars!"

"It's right here, Mrs. Brosius." She held out her King James Version Bible, and there, to my horror, the unlikely word stared back at me from Acts 12:4. I had used the New King James Version while preparing my lesson, and instead of "Easter," it read "Passover."

The students around Naomi perked up when they heard the offer of money. "Look, it's in my Bible, too!" Everyone who had access to a King James Bible greedily demanded a thousand dollars, until a savvy student, perhaps discerning the reality of my finances, suspiciously asked, "Is that going to be in US dollars?"

"Not necessarily," I quickly replied. Though I couldn't understand why a king in a Jewish city would be making Easter plans, I promised the students I would find out.

The next afternoon I came to class armed with the results of the previous evening's study. I learned that the word *pascha* appears twenty-nine times in the Greek New Testament. Twenty-eight times the KJV correctly translates it as *Passover*. Only once—in Acts 12:4—is it mistranslated "Easter," a form of Astarte, a Chaldean goddess.

My students groaned as they copied a page of notes based on *Strong's Exhaustive Concordance* and W. E. Vine's *Expository Dictionary of New Testament Words*.

"And now," I proclaimed, "it is time for me to pay Naomi and every student who found the word *Easter* in the Bible." I pulled out a bag of Nestle's 100 Grand Candy Bars, which the kids happily accepted in lieu of money I didn't have.

Whether students, teachers, pastors, or laypersons, we don't need to become fearful or upset when we encounter difficulties in a passage of scripture. Often understanding can be found by doing a little (or a lot!) of research.

And don't forget to sweeten the learning experience with a candy bar once in a while.

THE LOST TOOTH CLUB

Michelle Medlock Adams

I am creating something new. There it is! Do you see it?
I have put roads in deserts, streams in thirsty lands.
ISAIAH 43:19 CEV

As I watched Abby, my seven-year-old daughter, wiggling her loose tooth back and forth in her mouth, I smiled at her in the rearview mirror.

"You know, Abby, if you let me pull your tooth, you can stick it underneath your pillow tonight, and the Tooth Fairy will leave you a dollar!" I coaxed. "And you'll get to join the 'Lost Tooth Club.' "

Mrs. Chambers, Abby's first-grade teacher, had established the famous "Lost Tooth Club" many years before, and every child in Eagle Mountain Elementary knew about it. With every lost tooth, the students in Mrs. Chambers' class became members of the "Lost Tooth Club" and received stickers, pencils, and lots of other perks. It was a monumental moment for a first-grader.

Days passed and that poor, little tooth hung on for dear life. Abby carefully avoided the loose tooth while brushing her teeth. She refused to eat anything that required much chewing. And she was constantly wiggling it with her tongue.

Then, one night as I was loading the dishwasher, I heard, "My tooth! My tooth! Mom!"

I dashed down the hall and into Abby's room. There she stood, smiling a toothless grin and holding a sucker with a tooth stuck to it. It had fought a good fight, but that little tooth gave up the fight to a grape lollipop.

That night, Abby tucked the tooth under her pillow, and a Tooth Fairy wearing leopard-print slippers delivered the cash. The following day, Abby was inducted into the "Lost Tooth Club" and received all the goodies that went along with that special honor. Mrs. Chambers made a big deal of Abby's first tooth loss. It was exciting. From that day on, Abby checked her teeth daily, hoping to find another loose one.

Funny, isn't it? Abby had been so afraid to lose her tooth, but when the tooth finally lost out to a lollipop, Abby was thrilled to see it go because of all the benefits. Later, as I thought about Abby's loose-tooth experience, I realized that I had some "loose teeth" in my own life—things I was holding back from God—things I was afraid to let go. But when I finally did let go of those things in my life, God replaced them with better, stronger, and more beautiful ones—just like Abby's big, beautiful, white permanent tooth that replaced the old, weakened baby one.

So, I have a question for you: how are your spiritual teeth? If you're still walking around with a mouthful of worn-out baby teeth, it's time to let go and let God. It's time to join the celebrated "Lost Tooth Club" and enjoy the benefits of membership. Trust me; God gives better rewards than that leopard print slipper-wearing Tooth Fairy.

BEST-LAID PLANS OF MICE AND TEACHERS

Connie L. Peters

*Now listen, you who say, "Today or tomorrow we will go to
this or that city. . . ." Why, you do not even know what
will happen tomorrow. . . . Instead, you ought to say,
"If it is the Lord's will, we will live and do this or that."*
JAMES 4:13–15 NIV

Kathie believes learning should be fun, and through her thirty-one
years of teaching second graders, she lived by that philosophy.
When she taught about the solar system, she would string up the
planets from Mercury to Pluto. To demonstrate centrifugal force, she'd
whirl a bucket of water around in a vertical circle without spilling a
drop. From year to year, the kids would be amazed at this feat; until
one day the bucket hit the line upon which the planets hung, stopping
it in midair, dousing Kathie from head to toe. The kids sat there in
silence wearing can-we-laugh looks, mouths open, glancing at one
another. After the momentary shock, Kathie burst out laughing, and
her students joined in.

For President's Day, she dressed up as a headmaster, wearing her dad's black suit, her hair pulled tightly into a ponytail, and carrying a whip (dowel rod with black satin ribbon which snapped nicely). Usually cheery, Kathie spent the day with a grim expression. When her students misbehaved, they'd get a fake whipping, which sounded like the real thing. By the end of the day, they all wanted a whipping.

They had an old-fashioned spelling bee. Kathie asked one of the students to spell *car*. "Mr. Headmaster," the boy asked in keeping with the times, "what is a car?"

Kathie, trying to stay stone-faced, said, "It doesn't matter! Spell *car* anyway!" But she turned and giggled into her cloth handkerchief.

One day she was reading a story with enthusiasm when she noticed a mouse crawling into her lunch bag. So as not to upset her class, she kept reading but glanced over and noticed a second mouse joining his friend for lunch. This was too much. "Be quiet as mice," she told them. "I'll be back in a second." She dashed to the principal's office and told him about the infestation. "Please take care of this discreetly," she said. "I don't want to disrupt my class."

The principal agreed and followed Kathie into the classroom. Kathie continued the story, but to the children's amazement, the principal walked across the room and absconded with their teacher's lunch. And as he made his escape, two mice made theirs.

The class exploded into pandemonium. The principal grabbed a broom and chased the mice. "That way!" the students shouted or "Please don't hurt them!" After several minutes of running this way and that, the principal chased them out the door, down the hallway, and out the building.

Like the poet Robert Burns, Kathie found that best-laid schemes often go awry. You never know what you'll encounter in a day, especially when you're working with kids. That's why James instructs his readers to say, "If it's the Lord's will, we'll do this or that." Like Kathie, you strive for the best and learn to laugh when things go amuck. After all, a teacher's goal is not a perfect day, but for her students to discover and become who God designed them to be.

WARNING: DANGEROUS CONTENTS

Darlene Franklin

*Therefore let us keep the Festival, not with the
old bread leavened with malice and wickedness,
but with the unleavened bread of sincerity and truth.*
1 Corinthians 5:8 NIV

Science experiments often went awry during the years Dan Fritz
taught a self-contained classroom for fourth through sixth graders at
a children's home. Once he tried a recommended experiment involving
heating, cooling, and reheating water. He used the kind of dish the
instructions mentioned, but nowhere did it say to avoid doing it on the
stovetop. God kept him and his students safe when the dish exploded
into a thousand pieces.

Dan didn't expect the resulting mayhem when he planned an art
project for his middle school language arts class in a public school. He
had done this many times before.

At lunch, Dan enlisted a few students to prepare paint for their
afternoon's projects. Dan raided the art supply cabinet for tempera

paint powder, choosing bright, bold colors—red, blue, yellow, green, black, and white. He showed the students the correct proportion of water to paint. They could do it. After all, he had done this hundreds of times before. No reason to expect any problems.

When he opened the container holding blue powder, the contents did smell a little odd. He sniffed the air and decided maybe he was noticing the chop suey on the menu that day. He measured out the powder, mixed in water, and. . .

The blue surface bubbled and then fizzed before the paint exploded from the jar like a lava flow, spewing in every direction.

The blue volcano coated Dan's face, soaked the two students, and spattered against the two nearest walls.

Poor Dan not only had to clean up the mess, he had to pinch hit with a different lesson plan for a class starting in less than half an hour. He couldn't hide his mistake; anyone who saw him knew what had happened.

Later conversations with other teachers revealed that the tempera powder came in dated containers. If Dan had checked, he would have chosen a different jar. If he had paid attention to the foul odor, he could have avoided the explosion.

But Dan ignored the smell. He didn't know to check the date. The bad powder remained in the can waiting for an unsuspecting teacher, inert as long as it remained in its pure state.

Disaster only struck when someone mixed the powder with water. The powder tainted every molecule of water until it exploded out of the jar, leaving nothing behind.

The apostle Paul makes the same point about leaven. When a cook adds leaven to bread, the entire dough rises. If we ignore the warning signs and engage in malice and wickedness, sin acts the same way on us. It affects every part of our lives. Pure powder would have produced a useful product. Sincerity and truth work the same way in the unleavened dough of our lives. We would do better to follow the pattern given about unleavened bread during the festival of Passover, and search ourselves diligently for sin.

Let's be careful what paint powder we mix with our everyday actions.

NEW CLOTHES

Renae Brumbaugh

Be made new in the attitude of your minds; and to put on the new self,
created to be like God in true righteousness and holiness.
EPHESIANS 4:23–24 NIV

I've never known a student who purposely tried to look bad on the first day of school. On the first day, every student seems to wear his or her newest, nicest clothes. Many purchase special outfits just for the occasion. Others spend hours choosing from their existing wardrobes, ironing and making everything just right. If they'd only spend as much time on their homework as they do on their first-day outfits, they'd all be straight-A students.

Doesn't it feel great to wear a new outfit? I don't know about you, but whenever I have new clothes, I feel special. I feel sparkly and fresh, simply because I'm not wearing the old things that have been in my closet for years. It would be foolish of me to wear my old, faded things when I have beautiful new things to wear.

Yet, that's what I do much of the time. Oh, I'm not talking about my physical clothes. I don't have the fanciest wardrobe in the world, but I do try to look presentable. But when it comes to my spiritual "clothes," I often wear old rags. God doesn't want me dressing like a pauper. He's provided a beautiful new mental wardrobe in just my size, so I can dress like royalty.

Friends, God wants us to take off those rags! Throw them in the trash and burn them. We have something better, something sparkly and new. Why would we choose to wear old, stained, faded things when we have beautiful new things to wear? Why do we cling to our faulty, faded, worn-out way of thinking, when God has offered us a new way of life?

God is the King of kings and Lord of lords. We all know that royalty has the very best, the very finest. When we become His children, He wants us to *look* like His children! He wants us to dress ourselves as royalty. When we continue to live like we did before we knew Him, it's like wearing faded hand-me-downs when He's provided only the finest new garments.

As children of God, we need to clothe ourselves with love. We need to display kindness and compassion. The more we read His Word, the more we stay on our knees in prayer, the more we'll know His thoughts. As we become familiar with His thoughts and His ways, we'll find that our thoughts and ways will naturally, gradually reflect Him.

God loves us more than anything. He wants only the very best for His children. He has offered us that, but it's up to us to take it. We make the choices each day about what our minds and souls will wear. We can dig through the rag box and dress like paupers, or we can take advantage of the finery He's laid out for us in His Word. I don't know about you, but I know which I prefer. . . .

RESISTING THE *EEWW!*

Gena Maselli

Do not let any part of your body become an instrument of evil
to serve sin. Instead, give yourselves completely to God,
for you were dead, but now you have new life. So use your whole
body as an instrument to do what is right for the glory of God.
ROMANS 6:13 NLT

Mommy, look!" my preschooler said in wonder, his hands cupped together.

I knew he had found something special. And judging from the gentleness of his actions, I could tell we had just adopted another "pet."

As a homeschool mom, I constantly look for ways to encourage my children's love of learning, and nothing is quite as enticing as the great outdoors. We have studied several garden creatures: moths, butterflies, earthworms, caterpillars, and even a few rain-soaked snails. Seeing my son's discovery was a joy.

Gingerly, he opened his hands to show me his treasure. I bent down, eager to see what he had found. In a flash, a small black bug that looked like a cross between a beetle and cockroach ran over and around his fingers. I froze.

"Can we keep it?" he pleaded.

My mind raced as I quickly tried to decide what to do. Should I follow my primal urge to grab the nearest shoe and beat the intruder into oblivion? Snails and worms are one thing, but cockroaches are quite another.

Or should I embrace the little fellow as our newest pet? If we kept it, what would we use for his home? *No way I'm putting a cockroach in a Mason jar with a hole-filled plastic wrap top*, I thought. *Maybe a fire safe with a sign that reads, "No Family Allowed!" but definitely not a holey jar. Maybe I'm taking my commitment to the role as natural science teacher too seriously!*

As I contemplated these questions, my first grader entered the room.

"Sissy, look!" my preschooler called.

My daughter joined her brother and peered into his hands. With one peek, her face contorted. *"Eeww!"*

"Now, Elliana," I began hypocritically, "Lyric found a pet. Be nice to him like he was when you found your snails."

Just then, the toilet flushed. I looked up to see Lyric walking out of the nearby bathroom, his hands swinging naturally at his side. "Lyric, where's your pet?"

"I flushed it."

So much for gentle. Lyric went on with his afternoon, not giving another thought to his beloved pet.

While I had spent time considering whether to embrace the small invader, my daughter had called it like it was. An *eeww*. And when she responded accordingly, my son had recognized it for what it was, too.

How often do we consider accepting "bugs" into our lives, those things that are less than we deserve, instead of seeing them for what they are and saying, *"Eeww!"* There's nothing cute or lovable about ungodly things, and when we flush them out of our lives, we're definitely better off.

Tales from the Teacher's Lounge: Humor

I have never let my schooling interfere with my education.

MARK TWAIN

HOLIDAY LIBRARY HUMOR

Deborah Bates Cavitt

A merry heart doeth good like a medicine.
PROVERBS 17:22 KJV

Our elementary library celebrated holidays and celebrations throughout the year.

In September, we placed a huge paper tree on a wall in the auditorium. Each student wrote the name of the book he or she was reading on a paper leaf. The leaves were fall colors. After three to four hundred leaves were on the tree, it was beautiful. Many parents came in to take pictures.

In October, we displayed two giant posters of *Charlotte's Web*. The saying on one poster was, "Don't get caught in the web; bring your books back on time." The other poster read, "Don't get caught in the web; remember to use your good manners on the computer."

In November, we placed a giant turkey on the auditorium wall. This time each child cut out his or her handprints on papers of fall colors. Each child wrote his or her name and how many books he or she had read so far.

In December, the library was decorated. At each corner of the ceiling tiles was a two-foot hanging garland. The students usually chose the colors. My husband and custodians hung them. Posters were made that said, "Give the gift of reading during this holiday season."

Second semester, we had old Avon statues of George Washington and Abe Lincoln on display. On Valentine's Day, the kindergarteners made heart-shaped posters with old valentine cards and shapes glued on them. We hung these up, too. I put plastic eggs on each library shelf. Sometimes, they had a research question in them.

Then there was a day I will never forget. Usually I had back-to-back thirty-minute classes when it was check-out day. Several teachers came to me and asked for just fifteen minutes to check out. They were busy. Some teachers that were scheduled on a different day wanted to check out, too. So without looking up very often from my computer, I checked out nonstop for hours.

When it was time for lunch, I got up from my desk and noticed something strange. Every book from the nonfiction shelves was gone. There weren't any books until the 600s. That meant every 000–499 had been checked out. The other shelves hadn't been touched.

The last hour and a half before school was out, the students returned their books. One by one, the books were back in order the way they were supposed to be on the shelves. Before each class left, they said in unison, "April Fool's, Mrs. Cavitt."

MR. CUTLER, MY FIFTH-GRADE JOKESTER TEACHER

Deborah Bates Cavitt

If it is serving, then serve; if it is teaching, then teach; if it is to encourage, then give encouragement; if it is giving, then give generously; if it is to lead, do it diligently; if it is to show mercy, do it cheerfully.
ROMANS 12:7–8 NIV

When people ask me which were my favorite years in school, I usually say, "fifth grade and eleventh grade." My junior year was a favorite because I had a best friend, speech team, date, and prom.

In fifth grade I attended Godsman Elementary in Denver, Colorado. Mr. Cutler was my teacher. The first thing he told us was that he wasn't related to our fourth-grade teacher, Mrs. Cutler.

We thought he was kidding, but he wasn't. Looking back, he was too old for her anyway.

He loved to play jokes on other teachers. When it was Valentine's Day, he arranged for the entire school to parade through Mr. Valentine's classroom. Each of us had to say, "Happy Valentine's, Mr. Valentine." Mr. Cutler belly laughed when our class marched through. It was contagious, because all of us were laughing before we left the room.

I told Mr. Cutler and the class I was getting eyeglasses. I was so afraid to wear them. Mr. Cutler reassured me that I would make better grades and see the blackboard better. He had glasses and told us he was much better looking because of them. He made me promise not to put them on until he could put them on me.

The following week, I had my beautiful blue case with my eyeglasses inside. Mr. Cutler had me come to the front of the class. With his back to the class, he put my glasses on me. Mine were brown, points at the sides with crystals surrounding the eyes. Before Mr. Cutler turned around, he reached into his pocket and put his glasses on. Then he turned around. He had one of those disguise glasses with the big nose on. "Class, who do you think is better looking now?" No one answered because of the laughter. Both Mrs. Cutler and Mr. Valentine came in to see about the commotion. They left laughing.

Then there was the biggest joke of all. I think it was on me, too.

We always had a practice spelling test on Wednesdays. I looked forward to these days because if anyone got all the words right, he or she didn't have to take the test on Fridays. Most of the students were allowed to draw or read a book during the test. We had to be quiet. Not me. I was always chosen to give the test.

Mr. Cutler would sit at the back of the room at the reading table during the test. At the time, I didn't see the whole picture. You see, while he was at the reading table, Mr. Cutler was drinking coffee, grading papers, and writing in his grade book. Here I thought he was doing me a favor, and I was actually doing him a favor. I hadn't realized the implications until I received my teacher and librarian certification. Back then, teachers didn't get a long planning period. Maybe that's why I'm so grateful that Mr. Cutler helped me become a teacher and librarian.

FINGER WORK

Kathy Douglas

When I look at the night sky and see the work of your fingers—
the moon and the stars you set in place—what are. . .
mere human beings that you should care for them?
PSALM 8:3–4 NLT

From before birth, we make use of our fingers. With sonography and other medical-imaging techniques, preborn infants can be seen sucking on fingers or a thumb in their mother's womb. Those who work with premature infants encourage hand-to-mouth coordination in these babies so they learn to console themselves under stress. Some babies won't have anything to do with a pacifier. Give them their thumb, or three fingers jammed into their mouths, or nothing.

We buy our growing infants books with textured pictures to feel softness or roughness. As crawlers start investigating the world on their own, we have to watch what their fingers pick up. Moms look for nutritious "finger foods" for their toddlers, while trying to keep those exploring fingers out of the dog's dish or the cat litter.

What mother hasn't said or (more likely) yelled, "Get your fingers away from that stove!"? And who hasn't used fingers to teach small children their first songs—like, "Where Is Thumbkin" and others?

In preschool or kindergarten, finger painting begins before children use colored markers or paintbrushes, (unless, of course, those little fingers already got a hold of some type of writing utensil and experimented with it on the wall at home first). Children learn innumerable lessons with and through their fingers.

Diann, who has taught in a public grade school for years, makes good use of these finger facts as she teaches her first graders use of the "two finger rule" to properly space their words on a page.

"When you do your paper, make sure you have two finger spaces between your words," she tells her class. It's a good rule that has served her and her colleagues well over the years. The fingers of first graders are just the right size to make word spacing clear on their wide-lined yellow papers. It's a perfect, easy rule to remember and follow.

God is Spirit, but the Bible speaks often of God's *finger work*. God is so big that the psalmist wrote that the creation of the stars and moon is finger work for Him. (See verses above.) When the Egyptian magicians saw the miracles performed by the Lord God through Moses, they exclaimed, "This is the finger of God" (Exodus 8:19). Later, Christ told His critics that He drove out demons by "the finger of God" (Luke 11:20).

We can make no mistake about God's glorious might and power when we consider His finger work. But sometimes children may not understand a teacher's "finger work" spacing instructions. Even if it is a "perfect, easy rule to remember and follow."

Diann discovered her finger spacing instruction had been taken literally by one of her students. As she graded papers, the seasoned teacher found herself looking at a work of art in her stack of papers. A little girl in her class had meticulously drawn two fingertips—with each nail colorfully "polished"—between every word.

ALWAYS READY

Roberta Tucker Brosius

"It's like a man going away. He leaves his
house and puts his servants in charge. . . .
You do not know when the owner. . .will come back. . . .
He may come suddenly. So do not let him find you sleeping.
What I say to you, I say to everyone. 'Watch!' "
MARK 13:34–37 NIrV

Joey had missed out on high school. Like many classmates at the small Bible institute, he had spent his teen years abusing drugs and alcohol. Now living changed lives, these men and women eagerly pursued their education. Their enthusiasm and gratitude was compensation enough for their volunteer Language Arts instructor, me.

In my weekly public speaking class, I enjoyed Joey's Brooklyn accent—it would have made a dialect coach salivate. The students displayed individuality and creativity, especially during their demonstration speeches. One man showed how to diaper a baby, using his own infant. A retired navy cook made delicious cream puffs shaped like swans. A young woman demonstrated a manicure, using a classmate.

Joey hinted that his performance would trump the others and

requested that his speech on fire prevention be delivered outside, despite the winter weather. He warned that his demonstration would be unsafe in the classroom. I suspected that in his exhibition he would reference "Greta," the monstrous boiler in the basement of the old brick building. As his on-campus job, Joey tended the temperamental giant. The class and I anticipated the following week when he would declare the safety lessons learned from Greta.

Unfortunately, an ice storm arrived the day of our next session, and I couldn't risk the fifteen-mile drive to class. Unbelievably, the next week it snowed, and again I couldn't travel. Finally, the third week the weather cooperated.

The students and I huddled in the frosty air, listening to Joey's speech. What large item was under the blue tarp? Obviously Joey remembered my instruction to keep his visual supporting material out of view until the appropriate time. Finally, after informing us of the hazards inherent in boilers, he whisked away the tarp to reveal a small-scale model of Greta's brick home.

"And if you don't follow the proper precautions. . ." Joey's fiddled with something in his hands.

BOOM!

I screamed and jumped back, as the model exploded into flames. The sound of the crackling fire mixed with the laughter of the other students, who had known about Joey's planned inferno.

Afterward, I learned that Joey had set up his model and explosives the day of the ice storm to prepare for my arrival. When I didn't come, he dismantled it. The day of the snowstorm he prepared again, dragging out all the paraphernalia, and again had to tear it down and stow it. He joked that he would have detonated the model this week whether

I came or not.

Scripture urges us to be prepared not only for Christ's arrival, but also to live as His followers. Paul writes that God has already prepared good works for us to do—so let's be prepared to do them (Ephesians 2:10). And Peter urges us to be ready to gently explain our hope in Christ to anyone who asks (1 Peter 3:15).

Be prepared. Joey demonstrated it. We should live it.

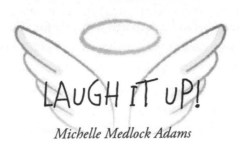

LAUGH IT UP!

Michelle Medlock Adams

A merry heart does good, like medicine,
but a broken spirit dries the bones.
PROVERBS 17:22 NKJV

"All the single ladies. All the single ladies. All the single ladies. All the single ladies. All the single ladies. All the single ladies. All the single ladies," spoke Mr. K. in his most dramatic voice. "Now put your hands up. Up in the club. . ."

As Mr. K. continued, pausing between each of the lyrics for a more theatrical effect, the students in his composition class broke into laughter. But they remembered his lesson about the power of words and the importance of choosing meaningful words when crafting their next composition. And when they remembered it, you can bet they remembered it with a smile. Mr. K. knows an important secret— laughter and learning go hand in hand.

It's no wonder why Mr. K. is so popular with the students. Every year in my hometown high school yearbook, the students choose "favorites"—favorite couple, favorite fashion trend, favorite saying, etc. Also included in the list of favorites is "Favorite Teacher," and year after year, Mr. K. wins. I asked my daughters, who are current high school students, why he is always chosen, and both said, "Because he is so funny!" A good sense of humor goes a long way with teenagers, and actually, a good sense of humor is an endearing quality no matter the age group. Bottom line, people of all ages love to laugh and apparently, we all *need* to let out a few belly laughs every day.

The Bible says that laughter is medicine to the body, and science backs up that claim. According to an article found on webmd .com, researchers have discovered that laughter increases blood flow, strengthens the immune system, lowers blood sugar, decreases pain, burns calories, reduces stress, and encourages more peaceful sleep—to name a few benefits.

So go ahead. Laugh it up and encourage others to laugh with you. That's another great thing about laughter—it's contagious! Find ways to bring joy to every situation—especially when you're teaching. Why do you think gifted public speakers usually open with a joke? Because it's endearing. People laugh with you, causing them to like you more. After they like you, they'll be more open to what you have to say—even if it's regarding verb conjugations or math equations. So take it from Mr. K., using humor on a daily basis is a great way to interject joy in the midst of learning. Joy is such a good thing. In fact, the Word of God says that "The joy of the Lord is our strength." Just think, you might be voted the favorite teacher of your school next year. And, even if you're not, you'll be laughing too hard to notice.

Confessions of a Substitute:
Trust

Optimism is the faith that leads to achievement;
nothing can be done without hope and confidence.

HELEN KELLER

GETTING TO THE BOTTOM OF THINGS

Shelley R. Lee

But it is a spirit in man, and the breath
of the Almighty gives them understanding.
JOB 32:8 NASB

I was subbing in an autism unit. It took some getting used to. There were children from varying levels of functionality, each needing specific types of help with one-on-one classwork and also during free play.

One little boy was very athletic and did somersault after somersault during free play. He was flipping around and landing on his feet and bottom, all with great agility. I thought about teaching him a cartwheel but decided that might not be a good idea. Just when I thought this, he did a cartwheel on his own. I obviously did not have all the information about this boy; he was very capable!

Another boy would stand in the corner and shriek if the lights were on or if anything flickered or reflected from the sun onto the walls. We would have to distract him with something else that didn't flicker or reflect.

Yet another boy just couldn't keep his pants from falling down. We would find them on the gym floor not far from where he was running and playing, and put them back on him. None of this bothered him in the least, as far as we could tell.

Each student had his or her own unique abilities and needs. As a substitute for the class, it took me some time to get all the information straight for each child.

At the end of the day we were each assigned one or two children to get to the bus, depending on their needs. I had a solidly built eight-year-old boy who did not speak. I helped him get his bulky winter coat on, then a harness for the bus ride over top of it, and lastly, a backpack on his shoulders. I held his hand as we carefully maneuvered down a couple flights of stairs. The swishing sound from his coat and gear accompanied his perplexed face and sluggish body. I continued to hold his hand as he moved slowly but steadily in the direction of the bus along with the other students and adults.

When we reached the bottom of the stairs I was met by the face of one of the teachers suppressing her laughter and then, when she tried to speak, not suppressing it. "His pants have fallen down!"

There he stood holding my hand, safe at the bottom of the stairs, with his pants at his feet. We helped him get put back together and then on the bus, and then all had a good laugh about it. Thankfully, no one seemed affected by the incident.

I clearly did not have all the information. I was so busy trying to keep this poor, overloaded Eskimo from falling that I did not know what was happening on the way down the stairs.

Sometimes you have to get to the bottom of things to understand.

HOLDING

Shelley R. Lee

"Put your ear to the earth—learn the basics. Listen—the fish in the ocean will tell you their stories. Isn't it clear that they all know and agree that God is sovereign, that he holds all things in his hand—every living soul, yes, every breathing creature?"

JOB 12:8–10 MSG

I was subbing as a teacher's aide in a children's correctional facility one day. The reasons for each of the students being there were varied and based on a myriad of circumstances. The mixture of students in this particular class ranged from true disabilities to behavioral issues having to do with their family life.

This held all the promise of an eventful day, to be sure, and I quickly saw that it was going to deliver.

We hadn't even gotten to attendance time yet, just unpacking and getting to the desks, and students were already upset. Someone's parent had forgotten to complete a form that needed to be returned so the student could participate in an upcoming event. Two boys were bantering rather seriously over another matter and needed some mediation.

One of the class aides—a large, strong man—went over to talk with them and redirect them away from one another. I soon learned the value of this man in the room.

When the students were finally at their desks for attendance and lunch count, they were challenging the teacher, who was clearly familiar with their drill. Many did not have their homework done, and one of the bantering boys was voicing his strong opinion about the work. When he would not stop complaining and distracting the rest of the class, the strong man had to take this boy to a desk in the back of the room, then shortly after that, out to a desk in the hall.

The boy was given clear boundaries and an easy way to stay within them, but he kept choosing to cross the line. He ended up out in the hall for most of the morning, then for a while, based on better behavior, was allowed back into the classroom.

That's when he lost it. Something seemed to snap and he went wild, attempting to physically harm another student. The strong man swiftly picked up the flailing boy and scooped him into a basket hold.

I was a little alarmed, but one of the other aides informed me that they were all trained to hold an out-of-control student like that until they could get the child to a place that was safe for the rest of the students. The strong man calmly asked the boy, holding him tightly as his hands and feet wiggled, "Do you want to stop here and cooperate?"

"No!" the boy yelled defiantly, with not a hint of compliance.

"Okay," said the strong man, and he took him out in the hall in his big arms until the boy calmed down and was able to return to the class.

The above memory came back to me Sunday in church when we were singing, "He holds the universe. He holds everyone on earth." I was thinking how God truly holds each of us, all of us, even the screaming ones who are incredibly sad and broken. He holds us tight even when we are rebelling or we are angry and just don't understand why life is so harsh. He holds us, each one, no matter what.

CHINCHILLA CONSEQUENCE

Shelley R. Lee

*From the Lord you will receive the reward of the inheritance. It is the
Lord Christ whom you serve. For he who does wrong will receive the
consequences of the wrong which he has done, and that without partiality.*
COLOSSIANS 3:24–25 NASB

W e let the chinchilla out every day, Mrs. Lee," said the students
in science class. I wasn't so sure I could believe them, but I told
them if they did their class work and we had no issues that maybe at
the end of class we could do that.

I'm not afraid of too many animals; I'm fascinated by them actually,
and this one looked harmless. So I weighed the possibilities too lightly,
in retrospect, and let them turn him loose at the end of class.

They were really a good group of kids. It would be fine. I thought.

But right out of the gate, the stuffed animal turned ninja-chinchilla
and jumped at a student while making a hissing-type noise. That was
the first indicator that, indeed, the students were *not* allowed to let the
chinchilla out of its cage, at any time, let alone every day.

It started running frantically across the room under desks and
scampering under students who were jumping up in the air to avoid
the crazed critter.

"You guys!" I yelled.

"Yeah, we're actually allowed to *feed* it every day," said one guilt-ridden student who now didn't want to get in trouble.

"We have to catch it quickly," I said, noticing that the bell would be ringing in a little over a minute.

One young man began taking control of the situation and directed the students to surround the animal. "Don't corner him, you guys," he said calmly.

Just then, the chinchilla spit at him, and then he recoiled in a funny combination of laughter and fear.

A couple of students now had small boxes they had found in the back of the room and were trying to lure the spitter in, while other students (the ones who weren't standing on their chairs) strategically placed themselves as roadblocks to help salvage the situation they had created.

I looked at the ticking clock, realizing that in less than a minute another twenty-five students would be filing into that room from the over-crowded hallway. . .and expect to walk past a chinchilla *in his cage*.

"Come here, little guy," coaxed one of the students. And somehow, it listened.

"Got him!" said the young man, carefully carrying one box covered by another box to the animal cage at the front of the room. He got the harried chinchilla back in his cage with the door shut behind him just before the bell sounded, and you could hear a collective sigh as the students offered faces of regret mixed with little grins. And we all went on with our day smiling more broadly as we parted.

Thankfully the students were able to remedy the consequence of their little lie, and no one was harmed (nor was any chinchilla harmed in the making of this story). If only all of life's consequences could be smoothed out so easily!

THERE'S ALWAYS HOMEWORK

Shelley R. Lee

Get along among yourselves, each of you doing your part. Our counsel is that you warn the freeloaders to get a move on. Gently encourage the stragglers, and reach out for the exhausted, pulling them to their feet. Be patient with each person, attentive to individual needs.
1 THESSALONIANS 5:13–14 MSG

During a long-term substitute teaching assignment, I taught English for three months. My oldest son, Trevor, was one of my freshmen students each day, and let's just say, he wasn't always the most academically energized pupil you've ever met.

As a natural result of this job, I had to keep tabs on his grades continually as I entered his assignments into the grade book. He hated this of course.

When it came time to turn in homework assignments to receive credit, he now passed his up to the front of the class with everyone else. I noticed there were no longer blank spaces in the grade book as there had been in previous months next to his name.

At home in the evenings when backpacks hit the floor by the door and, exhausted, everyone would gather for food, I would ask all four of my sons who had homework. Trevor's standard answer was that he didn't have any. I would frequently remind him of an assignment due in a week or a test coming up.

"Just because it's not due tomorrow doesn't mean you don't have homework," I offered.

He looked blankly at me as if I were from an unknown dimension. His hiding from the homework gig was coming to a close and he was defenseless, for three months of English class anyway.

Without a lot of noticeable effort his grade improved dramatically that semester from a low C to an A, in English anyway.

His good friend Chris, who consistently earned high grades, thought for sure that I was skewing the grading for Trevor. Chris would joke with me about it. Leaning over my desk, "You're helping him out, right?" he would ask. "You know. . ."

He let the end of his sentence trail out as he pointed to the grade book with a sly grin.

"Chris, no, I wouldn't do that," I said. "It's just that Trevor can't get away with anything right now. He has to put the assignment papers in my hands, and he can no longer tell me he doesn't have homework, because I know."

That was eight years ago, and recently, Chris reminded me of those days, laughing heartily. "Remember when you gave Trevor an A in English because you were our sub?" He really wasn't sure he could believe that simple accountability was what did the trick.

Yet, it is true. The power of simple encouragement, helping each other, building one another up, is powerful. It calls us all out to live up to higher standards, not out of guilt, but because someone who cares is watching.

STRESSED OUT!

Shelley R. Lee

*When the Lord brought back the captive ones of Zion, we were
like those who dream. Then our mouth was filled with laughter
and our tongue with joyful shouting; then they said among
the nations, "The Lord has done great things for them."*

PSALM 126:1–2 NASB

I am a regular substitute teacher in my school district. It is an interesting job that changes every day, and it brings so much laughter to my life. Children bring joy that is beautifully pure and unexpected.

One day in a physical education class, I was running along the perimeter of the gym with the children at the start of the period. Some were strong and sure, others tired and halting. I was offering encouragement to them as we circled at different paces.

When we had our five minutes of cardio in I announced, "It's time to stretch out."

"We're already stressed out!" yelled one little girl with an appalled face.

"Stretch, honey. We're going to stretch," I clarified.

"Oh, okay," she said, plopping down like a happy rag doll on the creaking floor, apparently quite relieved that she was no longer being commanded to stress. Phew! Stretching was a much better option.

I laughed for a bit, mostly to myself, but a residual smile continued on my face through much of the morning.

I thought later about how quickly that little girl's attitude changed when she had a view of a more pleasant option. She was no longer thinking on the unpleasantries of life, for which there seem to be no shortage even for little girls, unfortunately.

There is much in life to celebrate and be joyful about, and thankfully, we don't have to stress out just because someone tells us to, or we think they told us to. We do get to choose to see the blessings in the great mix of things.

Best of all, if we are in a seriously stressful place, we know our Rescuer is on His way, and we will celebrate at some point, somehow. It may not look as we expect it to, and at times, it may be just as simple as a happy time to plop on the floor and stretch. Not stress.

SUBSTITUTE TEACHING
AND SINKING SHIPS

Michelle Medlock Adams

"For I know the plans I have for you," declares the Lord, "plans to prosper you and not to harm you, plans to give you hope and a future."
JEREMIAH 29:11 NIV

Jeff and I had prayed about it and felt it was the right thing to do. So I spent the next two months preparing to launch out into the world of full-time freelance writing. Giving up the regular paycheck I had been earning as a magazine writer was difficult and scary, yet my books and my speaking were beginning to take up so much of my time that I could no longer do it all. Plus, I had three regular clients and several magazine writing opportunities—I was set. All was well with the world. . .or so I thought.

The month after quitting my nine-to-five job, one of my regular clients moved three states away and no longer needed my writing assistance. My second client let me know that he still needed my help but only once every quarter. And my third client, who was my biggest payer, informed me that he and his wife were divorcing, which was bad on several levels since his ministry was a marriage reformation ministry. Obviously, he no longer needed a ministry newsletter since his ministry folded. Thus, I was forced to substitute teach while scrambling to rebuild my freelance writing client base.

I filled out the substitute teacher paperwork and waited by the phone the first day I was eligible to teach. To my surprise, I got a call! They needed me to substitute teach at an area middle school—seventh grade. Scary.

"Okay, I can do this," I muttered as I climbed the stairs to my assigned classroom.

The first four periods went pretty well, although I was bored out of my mind. Then after a brief lunch at my desk, I was back to work.

"Is Larissa here today?" I asked, scanning the room.

"Larissa?" I called more loudly. "I need you to gather your belongings and head to room 320 to retake a test."

"I'm here," said a gruff voice from the back of the room. "But I ain't going to take no test, and you can't make me. You ain't even a real teacher."

"Well," I said, fake smiling. "I am your teacher for today, so please get your things and go to room 320—now."

"I ain't going," she said, staring me down.

Like any savvy substitute, I called for backup. Miss Larissa did go to room 320, and I just wanted to go home. I never realized how long 8:00 a.m. to 3:30 p.m. could feel.

Yes, I had launched out into the sea of freelancing and my ship had started to sink; however, God was still my captain and after only a few weeks, my freelance plate was once again full. I only had to substitute five more times. It's during those "sinking seasons" that we have to keep our eyes of faith wide open and our hearts full of expectancy. Just remember: God has a plan for each one of us, and it's a good plan. I'm thankful my plan only included a few days of substituting.

A Teacher's Homework:
Love

No man can be a good teacher unless he has feelings of warm affection toward his pupils and a genuine desire to impart to them what he believes to be of value.

BERTRAND RUSSELL

GATHERING BITS OF FUZZ

Anita Higman

She speaks with wisdom, and faithful instruction is on her tongue.
PROVERBS 31:26 NIV

When my son, Scott, was a little guy he had a fish tank in his room, like many children enjoy. Fish are among the core components of childhood. But before long, one of those core components escaped from the tank and landed behind the chest of drawers. Pretty dramatic situation for a fish! For humans, the experience would liken to being catapulted from a cruise ship and landing in the water!

Scott and I frantically moved the furniture to retrieve the poor thing. The fish had gone into hysterics, flopping about on the carpet, gathering bits of fuzz on his fins. We gingerly picked him up and slipped him back into his watery world, fuzz and all. We assumed this incident would be the beginning of the end for fishy, but amazingly, that fish survived much longer than we ever imagined. He was one tough fish.

That is the way high school feels—like that same fish flinging itself around in a new place where he didn't feel he belonged and where he felt like he would surely perish without a helping hand. Yep, that's high school. But thanks to the mercies of God, I had a teacher in high school who became that helping hand. I'll call her dear Mrs. Brier. I don't know what I would have done without Mrs. Brier's help—her compassion, caring, and generosity of spirit! She was a lifesaver, picking me up gingerly, after I'd been flapping around, not doing anything more remarkable than picking up fuzz.

Then one summer God's mercies were offered to me again in the form of a job; Mrs. Brier hired me to work in the school library. She watched over my work, but she also had great faith that I could get the job done. I was fortunate enough to be able to spend some time with Mrs. Brier, and I suppose I was always watching her, observing her, even when I wasn't conscious of it. You see, I was in desperate need of a role model—someone with maturity and grace and self-control—and she had those qualities in abundance.

Looking back, I believe Mrs. Brier held to Proverbs 31:26 better than anyone I've ever known. Truly, she did speak with wisdom, and faithful instruction was indeed on her tongue. And it made a big difference in all the lives she touched. Especially mine.

As I grow older I pray that I can be like the wise and noble Mrs. Brier. I hope, too, that even though I'm not a teacher, I can reach out to people and be God's helping hand like she was to me. If I can do all of that—and it's a lot—then I'll feel as though I lived my life well and that I would make Mrs. Brier proud.

PLENTY OF THE GOOD STUFF

Anita Higman

We have different gifts, according to the grace given us.
If your gift is prophesying, then prophesy in accordance with
your faith; if it is serving, then serve; if it is teaching, then teach;
if it is to encourage, then give encouragement.

ROMANS 12:6–8 NIV

Hugs—they are so warm and reassuring when they come from someone beloved. They are like snuggling into a cozy pile of clothes straight out of the dryer. Only much better. There's no lingering sock odor or static cling!

I know of a kindergarten teacher—I'll call her Nancy—who often gets smothered by those cozy hugs. Sometimes when Nancy stands in the hallway to visit with a parent or friend, a former student will rush up to her in a *whoosh* to give her a hug. It's the endearing kind of bear hug that seeps into the spirit as well as the tear ducts long after the hug is over. Nancy always reciprocates with a hug and a kind word. It's obvious that Nancy is loved by her students. So much so they remember her with affection years later! That level of admiration doesn't just happen. It is earned.

I can only imagine all the uplifting comments and enriching discussions that must have taken place in Nancy's classroom. Children can certainly listen better and learn more in an environment where they feel cared for. Kids are intuitive; they know when teachers value their opinion and enjoy their company. They know, and it matters greatly. Nancy must have been very aware of this truth, and like a pitcher of sweet lemonade, she stirred in plenty of the good stuff. No puckery brew for Nancy!

Over the years my daughter, Hillary, was also influenced by teachers who had this same kind of talent for encouragement. Hillary would sometimes leave for school with an *Anne of Green Gables* look of forlorn despair and then come home from school thrilled with the news of how a teacher had praised her work. One teacher wrote, "Great job, Hillary. When you're published someday I want an autographed book!" These teachers are like bright bobbing buoys—in a sometimes scary sea—called high school.

The many words and deeds over the years made a difference in Hillary's life. She came to believe she could accomplish good things, and she already has. My daughter will soon graduate from college with honors. I can't help but think that the caring attention and the encouraging words from teachers helped to mold her into the bright Christian young woman she is today.

God has much to say about this delightful—or maybe I should say *light-filled*—behavior. He says that encouragement has great value—that it's a gift of the Spirit. These teachers have that gift in abundance and, like people releasing confetti as the parade goes by, they cheerfully distribute inspiration at every opportunity. I thank God for their presence in the lives of these students, including the life of my own daughter.

It would be a good and lovely thing to remember a teacher who has changed your life or the life of your child. Even if we can't honor them with a parade we can cheer them on!

BOY CRAZY

Anita Higman

Let the wise listen and add to their learning,
and let the discerning get guidance.
PROVERBS 1:5 NIV

Okay I admit it—I was boy crazy in college. And now, of course, you'll want a full report of my escapades or at least a juicy morsel for illustration. I'll tell you this—when I went to the library to hit the books I wasn't always studying. Or even reading. I was busy positioning myself at the best possible table at the most flattering angle so that I could be seen by the cutest guys in school. I do realize now how ridiculous this sounds. But you should also know that my lack of discernment and maturity was not without its consequences.

Several times in college I got my heart broken. I was a basket case without the basket—I was left diminished and vulnerable in my emotions. After a few rounds in the dating ring it became apparent that I was falling in love much more easily than young men were falling in love with me. The routine went like this—I would go out with a nice Christian guy a few times, fall into what I thought was real love, and then when the young man said good-bye, I was devastated. Seems like

I heard the word *good-bye* a lot in college!

Once when I experienced a particularly bad case of heartsickness, I went to one of my favorite professors for counseling. This teacher—I'll shorten his name to Mr. M.—took the time out of his busy schedule to talk to me. But even though I cannot recall what Mr. M. said to me all those many years ago, I know he never made me feel unworthy of his time. I'm sure he must have comforted me by saying, "Anita, this too shall pass." I doubt I left that day skipping down the sidewalk, but I knew there was a teacher out there who cared enough to listen to my sad ramblings about boys and offer me advice on life and love.

It's hard not to wonder what God thought about my swooning back then. Was He shaking His head at me? Then again, perhaps God wasn't all that shocked about the way I adored cute college guys. After all, He was the one who'd *made* all those cute college guys. But I know God was glad that Mr. M. was there for me with a kind word and a map to find my way back home when I felt lost.

God must surely appreciate teachers with these qualities. They are His emissaries, His right-hand folks. The people who don't mind being in the trenches of life—getting a bit of grime on their spirits as they listen to the travails of their students. As they counsel each of them, they fulfill the scripture in Proverbs concerning guidance. And yes, this counsel even includes advising young women who are in great need of a little common sense about boys!

PINK WHIRLING CONFECTION

Anita Higman

And walk in the way of love, just as Christ loved us and gave himself up for us as a fragrant offering and sacrifice to God.
EPHESIANS 5:2 NIV

Her name is Ruth—and she was my professor in college—the one who cheered me on, touched my heart, and well, changed my life. Of course, I didn't call Ruth by her first name when she was my teacher, but over the years, that detail would change along with our relationship. Later in life I would come to call her by the endearing name of *Moddy*, because she became so much more to me than a professor. She became like a mom.

But I'm getting ahead of myself. Let me start at the beginning— that is, the years when I attended college. Moddy was adored by her students, and as the scriptures say, "She lived a life of love." In fact, love hovered around Moddy like the pink whirling confection in a cotton candy machine. She also gave off so many sparks of creative energy around the campus that she could have been her own traveling fireworks display! During that time, she invited me to her home and even treated me like part of the family. I can't imagine why, since I was an awkward, homely kid with dreams so obnoxiously big that I had to push them around in a wheelbarrow. But I was deeply grateful for Moddy's attention and maternal kindness.

After graduation, unfortunately, Moddy and I lost track of each other, but then years later miraculously, we found each other again. What joy! For months we wrote long letters. Yes, real mail—written on paper. Primitive, I know! We laughed and cried through our correspondence. The letters piled up—I think we wore out the postman—and I saved them in decorative boxes like the treasures they were. Over the months she gave me lots of motherly advice and helped me move on from some rough childhood experiences that were hard to let go. And, according to Moddy, I became like a daughter to her. She even calls me, "Little Love."

Our relationship blossomed all over again. Since we were both authors, it was only natural that we would consider writing a book together and perhaps sharing our unique relationship with others. And we did! In fact we wrote two manuscripts that were published.

Now, more years have come and gone, and Moddy has seen me through life's mayhem and merry delights, and I have seen her through the same. We have a snug-forever kind of relationship—"No matter the weather," she would always say.

Certainly not all teacher/student relationships turn out like ours. I never became mother/daughter close to any of my other teachers, but Moddy and I have such a sweet story to tell, it always feels right to share it.

Decades later, I'm still grateful for a teacher who continues to live a life of love—Moddy Ruth—who cheered me on, touched my heart, and well, changed my life forever!

KING TUT

Janice Hanna

But the Lord said to Samuel, "Do not consider his appearance or his height, for I have rejected him. The Lord does not look at the things people look at. People look at the outward appearance, but the Lord looks at the heart."

1 SAMUEL 16:7 NIV

The world history class I taught back in '99 provided the perfect creative outlet for this very artistic teacher. I decided to take a humanities approach. My students wouldn't just learn dates and wars. Oh no. With each time period we studied, they would learn the architecture, the foods, the music, the culture, and all applicable world-changing events. What fun! I had a blast putting together my room. You could literally walk the four walls, moving through the different eras. All along the way were pictures, copies of artifacts, and dozens of other things to make you feel like you'd actually gone back in time.

We started our year with Creation, of course. From there, we moved to the ancient world. Because I wanted to make the kids feel like they were a part of the story, I decided to invite King Tut to visit our classroom. Okay, so he wasn't the real King Tut. It was actually my husband, wrapped in toilet paper. (And boy, did it take some doing to talk him into this!) He arrived—walking quite slowly, of course—into the classroom. At first, the students couldn't stop laughing long enough to enjoy the presentation. By the time I finished interviewing the famous king, however, the kids in the class were thoroughly on board. They asked him a host of questions, and he responded with his quirky sense of humor.

King Tut left us that day, headed back to Ancient Egypt (or rather, back to work at the sheriff's office, where he wore a completely different sort of getup). My students grew up, moved on, but I'm sure they never forgot that encounter. I haven't forgotten, either. In fact, I think about that visit with the tightly wound king quite often. Something about him causes me to think a bit deeper, beyond the layers of toilet paper.

You know, what we see on the outside isn't always an indicator of what's on the inside, even with our students. And, as teachers, we're so busy. We have so much on our plates. Because things are so chaotic, we don't always take the time to see below the stiff exterior some of our students wear, to the soft heart inside. We don't take the time to unwrap the tightly wound layers.

Maybe the outside is crusty and hard. The expression is gruff. The tone is demeaning. But if we could peel back the layers, what would we find? Likely, a child full of wonder and curiosity, just waiting for someone to take a chance on him, to show him the way. . .a child wishing someone would take the time to investigate, to dig deeper.

The next time I think of King Tut, I hope I'm reminded of the thousands of students around the globe who are too scared to put their guard down. I also hope I remember to pray that they will land in classrooms where teachers take the time to unwrap them. . .one roll of toilet paper at a time.

PEOPLE WATCHERS

Janice Hanna

Suppose a brother or a sister is without clothes and daily food.
If one of you says to them, "Go in peace; keep warm and well fed,"
but does nothing about their physical needs, what good is it? In the
same way, faith by itself, if it is not accompanied by action, is dead.
JAMES 2:15–17 NIV

Years ago I taught creative writing at a local school of the arts. I had so much fun with my students, always thinking outside the box. Writing prompts were my thing. I used them regularly. And I was the queen of field trips, too. We took dozens over the years.

One memorable trip took us to the international terminal of the Houston airport. This was back in the day when you could actually go up to the gate, even if you didn't have a ticket. Each of my students had a notepad and pen. I situated them in various places and told them to "people watch." They did just that, taking great notes. I still remember watching my students act like spies, sneaking from place to place to get the best view of the scenes playing out in front of them.

And oh, what scenes! Lovers weeping as they parted ways. Mothers and fathers celebrating as they wrapped their arms around children and grandchildren they hadn't seen in years. Single women with babies, boarding planes all alone, with no one to help. Businessmen, with briefcases in hand, focused only on the task ahead. Flight attendants, weary and worn, pulling their rolling suitcases behind them. Janitors, emptying trash cans in the terminal.

If we paid attention, we saw it all. And what my students saw, they wrote down. I could see them scribbling and scratching in their writing tablets, many in a frenzy.

Afterward, we met together, where I instructed them to write a fictional story, based on what they'd seen. They came up with some great pieces—some pretty funny, and others quite serious. I could hardly believe how well this "writing prompt" had worked. Strange, how much you see when you actually pay attention.

I've thought about that exercise at the airport many times through the years. It triggers a deep, thoughtful response on my part. God wants us to be people-watchers. Oh, not in a weird, nosy sort of way, but in an observant sort of way. If we're really watching, we'll notice when that neighbor is going through a personal struggle. If we're watching, we'll pick up on the clues our coworker is giving as she walks through a divorce. When our focus is on those around us instead of just our own needs, we follow the clues. And we respond. True people watchers are empathetic and kind. They have the mind of Christ toward the person in pain.

We don't "people watch" so that we can tell stories about others. No, we should ask the Lord to give us His vision, His ears, and His heart for those in need.

The next time you're out among people, spend a little time asking the Lord to give you His love for them. Don't rush away, thinking only of your own story. Realize that each of them has a story, too. And maybe—just maybe—those two stories are supposed to merge, creating a whole new page in your writing tablet.

SOMEONE TO WATCH OVER ME

Janice Hanna

The righteous cry out, and the Lord hears them; he delivers them from
all their troubles. The Lord is close to the brokenhearted and saves
those who are crushed in spirit. The righteous person may have
many troubles, but the Lord delivers him from them all.
PSALM 34:17–19 NIV

Twelve sixteen-year-old girls in one classroom. That was my task for the year. Twelve hormonal, temperamental, quirky, fun girls, all gathered in one room to learn. . .from me. I made up my mind early in the year to use every trick in the book to keep them entertained and ready to learn. And when the director of our small Christian school approached me about putting on a Valentine's banquet, complete with entertainment from the girls, I jumped on board. Right away, I thought about Gershwin music. Perfect for a romantic evening entertaining the parents, and a great fund-raiser for our little Christian school, to boot.

Only one problem—not all of the girls were strong singers. Some were nominal, at best. Still, I felt sure they could handle it as a team.

At least half of the girls in the class could carry the weight for the rest, right? Sure. Everything would end well. I just knew it.

I started by purchasing a Gershwin songbook and auditioning the girls. Turned out most did a pretty good job, so I decided to give each girl her own solo. (Talk about living on the edge!) I did my best to tailor the solos to the girls, making sure the lyrics fit the students. Each girl seemed happy with her assigned number.

For weeks they rehearsed. They did so well that I decided to add choreography. Perfect! Finally the big night arrived. I'll never forget taking my place in front of them to direct. They looked amazing in their black pants, white tuxedo shirts, and red bow ties. Just perfect. One by one, they sang their solos—the girl who struggled with her grades, the one who fought to fit in with the rest of the group, the teen with the over-the-top attitude, the one who could barely hold a tune, the shy one, the one with serious emotional issues, the one with the lyrical voice.

They poured out their hearts through the moving words of those Gershwin tunes, and there wasn't a dry eye in the place.

Finally came the song I'd waited for all evening, my very favorite. As the lyrics to "Someone to Watch Over Me" rang out that night, I was reminded that God was, indeed, watching over us all. In that moment, I realized that His nearness—both to those girls and to me—was very real. His presence hovered over us, through the charming strains of a Gershwin melody.

What about you? Do you sense God's nearness? Can you feel His love, even when you don't feel like joining in the song? Have you ever pondered the fact that He's right there, watching over you? He's not standing at a distance. He's close enough to sweep you into His arms, to rescue you from your troubles.

Today, Someone—the great Someone—is watching over you. Rest easy. He's right there, ready to rescue and save.

CHEERLEADERS AND WIENER DOGS

Michelle Medlock Adams

*Therefore encourage one another and build
each other up, just as in fact you are doing.*
1 THESSALONIANS 5:11 NIV

When I was in first grade, Mrs. True made an announcement that would forever change my life.

"We're having a poetry contest this week," she said, "so use today and tomorrow to come up with your best poem." We had just studied the various types of poetry, and I decided I really liked the ones that rhymed.

As my classmates wrote about their parents, grandparents, aunts and uncles, brothers and sisters, I carefully crafted the words to my poem: "I Love Penny." Penny was my seven-year-old wiener dog and my best friend in the whole world. My poem went a little something like this: "Penny is my very best friend. I'll love her to the very end. She's a very special wiener dog. I love her though she smells like a hog. . ." Okay, so I wasn't exactly a first-grade Dr. Seuss, but my poem was good enough to win first prize. (I guess the other first-grade poets were really bad.) At any rate, I won a few sparkly pencils and the honor of going first in the lunch line. Mrs. True also displayed my poem in the front of the room for all to see. I felt very special.

Little did Mrs. True know that her lesson on poetry and subsequent contest was a turning point in my life. After winning that writing contest I thought to myself, "Hey, I am actually good at something. . . maybe I should do more of this writing stuff." And so I did. I started writing all the time. I wrote poems about every member of my family. I wrote short stories about two squirrels named Frank and Millie. I even became the editor of my elementary school newspaper, *The Panther Paw*. And all the while, Mrs. True was cheering me on. Today, when I make appearances for "Young Author's Day" at elementary schools and read my children's books to the students, I am always asked two questions: "How old are you?" (which I quickly skip over) and, "When did you become a writer?" Without missing a beat I always answer, "In first grade, when Mrs. True taught me about poetry and I won a contest for a poem about my big, fat wiener dog."

Teachers make such an impact on who we become as adults. They have a voice into our young, eager hearts, and that voice may be the only one that offers an encouraging word. I'm so thankful for Mrs. True and for teachers like her who challenge young people to follow their dreams. Though I am not a teacher in the school system, I often teach at writers' conferences, and I always ask God to help me be a "Mrs. True" in someone's life. Offering an encouraging word at the right time can be life-changing for someone. Why not be a "Mrs. True" in somebody's life today?

PINK CADILLACS AND ENCOURAGING WORDS

Michelle Medlock Adams

Everyone enjoys a fitting reply; it is wonderful
to say the right thing at the right time!
PROVERBS 15:23 NLT

I recently read a quote by Mary Kay Ash that said, "Don't limit yourself. Many people limit themselves to what they think they can do. You can go as far as your mind lets you. What you believe, you can achieve." I love that inspiring quote. Pretty in pink, Mary Kay Ash may have been the one who first spoke it, but those same words could have been credited to Mr. Ralston at Parkview Elementary in 1987.

When I was a senior in high school, I already knew that I wanted to pursue writing as a career. Writing had basically chosen me when I was only seven years old, but since that life-changing revelation, I'd been bombarded by guidance counselors and career planners who all urged me to have "a backup plan" in case the writing thing didn't work out for me. I'd never even considered a different career path until then, so I was very confused and worried. After much thought, I decided teaching would be my "backup plan," and so I signed up for a cadet teaching class through my high school. This meant that every morning, I would serve as a teacher's helper for my favorite sixth-grade teacher, Mr. Ralston. Morning after morning, I showed up in Mr. Ralston's classroom and graded papers for him. Sometimes, I even presented a lesson or two. It was fun, and the students seemed to like me, so I was surprised when it came time for my evaluation. Mr. Ralston looked me right in the eyes and asked, "Do you really want to teach?"

Had I really been that transparent?

"Don't misunderstand. You'll do fine in teaching," he continued. "But is your heart really in it?"

"Not really," I admitted. "I want to write. I want to write news stories and fiction and poetry and so much more. . .but I've been told it's tough to make it as a writer, so I thought maybe I would teach and then use my summers off to pursue writing."

As I shared with Mr. Ralston my hopes, my dreams, and my carefully plotted-out backup plan, he smiled and said, "Why are you preparing to fail with this backup plan? If you want to be a writer, go for it! Pursue writing!" Mr. Ralston's encouragement to follow my dreams was the little nudge I needed to help me push past my fears of not making it as a writer and simply, "Go for it!" No, Mr. Ralston didn't drive a pink Cadillac, but his words put me back in the driver's seat headed toward my destiny—the plan that God had for me—to be a writer.

That's what an encouraging word will do when spoken in love in due season—that's what the Word of God says. So, let's try and be like Mr. Ralston and speak that word of encouragement at just the right time and make a difference in someone's life today. Wearing pink is optional.

Teacher's Pet

Michelle Medlock Adams

Even before he made the world, God loved us and chose us in Christ to be holy and without fault in his eyes. God decided in advance to adopt us into his own family by bringing us to himself through Jesus Christ. This is what he wanted to do, and it gave him great pleasure.

<small>Ephesians 1:4–5 nlt</small>

Ally, my youngest daughter who is a junior in high school, has never been the kind of student who adores school. Sure, she makes good grades because she is competitive enough that she desires to do well in whatever she does; however, she never seems to enjoy it—until last year when she took chemistry. Mr. Schu, which is short for his real name, "Schulenburg," made chemistry interesting and fun for her, and she managed to do really well in his class because she studied extra hard. Surprised by her enthusiasm for chemistry, I asked Ally about her devotion to the class. Her response? "I don't want to disappoint Mr. Schu. He is so nice and tries really hard to make the class interesting."

This year, Ally needed a recommendation letter to gain early acceptance into her college of choice, and she asked Mr. Schu if he would endorse her. He came through big-time. As I read the words he wrote about my daughter, I teared up.

"Ally, honey," I said, "I think you may be the teacher's pet when it comes to Mr. Schu."

Ally smiled as she put the recommendation letter in her college folder.

Being the teacher's pet is such a good feeling. Seriously, who doesn't like to be the favorite? While we all can't be the favorite student in every "classroom" in life, we can all be Teacher's pets where God is concerned. The Bible tells us that we are the apple of God's eye. He adores us! He highly favors us! Bottom line, He loves us and nothing can separate us from His love. Romans 8:38–39 says, "And I am convinced that nothing can ever separate us from God's love. Neither death nor life, neither angels nor demons, neither our fears for today nor our worries about tomorrow—not even the powers of hell can separate us from God's love. No power in the sky above or in the earth below—indeed, nothing in all creation will ever be able to separate us from the love of God that is revealed in Christ Jesus our Lord" (NLT).

In other words, we didn't earn His favor or love, and we can't lose it. Be confident of this—God loves you. He isn't some mean old guy in the sky with a big stick ready to bop you on top of the head every time you make a mistake. He isn't mad at you. He is madly in love with you. He has a plan for your life and it's a good one, and He can't wait to show Himself big on your behalf. Just as my Ally had confidence to ask Mr. Schu for a letter of recommendation because she knew she had favor with him, you can present your requests to God, knowing that you have great favor with Almighty God. Think about that today—you are highly favored by the Creator of the Universe. You are the ultimate Teacher's pet!

BE A GIVER

Michelle Medlock Adams

> *Jesus said, "Let the little children come to me, and do not hinder them,
> for the kingdom of heaven belongs to such as these."*
> MATTHEW 19:14 NIV

When my girls were in elementary school, they couldn't wait to go shopping and pick out Christmas presents for their teachers—their homeroom teacher, music teacher, gym teacher, art teacher, the librarian and her assistant, the ladies in the attendance office, and of course, the principal. From giant tins full of gourmet popcorn to perfumed body lotions to boxes of chocolate—my girls knew just what to buy for each teacher.

This one particular holiday season, Abby and Ally helped me wrap each Christmas gift and excitedly carried all the gifts into Eagle Mountain Elementary on the last day of school before Christmas break. I thought we had covered all the bases, so to speak, but apparently we hadn't. Ally, who was in second grade at the time, realized as she was passing out the gifts to the women in the attendance office, that she hadn't brought a gift for Miss Rosie, the school custodian. Ally loved Miss Rosie because Miss Rosie always talked to Ally in the halls and made her feel special. Ally felt so bad about not buying Miss Rosie a present that she spent her lunch hour making a special Christmas card for the caring custodian, and then Ally taped her lunch money onto the Christmas card and handed it to Miss Rosie.

Minutes later, I received a phone call at home. I hoped it wasn't the office telling me that one of my girls had come down with the stomach bug that was going around, and I was happy when Miss Rosie assured me the girls were just fine. Still, I wondered why Rosie was crying. As she relayed the story to me, Rosie said she just couldn't believe a child could love her so much that she would give up her own lunch money and present it as a Christmas gift to her.

"I didn't want Ally to go without food today," Miss Rosie said, "but I didn't want to hurt her feelings by refusing her gift. So I sneakily bought a school lunch for her today. I watched her eat school pizza so she didn't go without. I wanted you to know that."

"Thank you so much for taking care of her," I said, touched by her story.

"No, thank *you* for having such a special daughter," Rosie continued. "Ally reminded me what Christmas is all about. I won't go into any details, but I really needed that reminder today."

As I hung up the phone, I praised God that He had given me such precious children. I praised Him for using Ally to touch Miss Rosie's heart. And I asked Him to help me be as sensitive to His leading as my Ally had been. I want to challenge you to pray that same prayer with me today, because you just never know when a "Miss Rosie" may cross your path and need to be reminded of God's infinite love.

FITTING IN

Connie L. Peters

To the praise of the glory of his grace, wherein he hath made us accepted in the beloved. In whom we have redemption through his blood, the forgiveness of sins, according to the riches of his grace.

EPHESIANS 1:6–7 KJV

Lorraine enjoyed teaching the six-year-old girls in her church's Wednesday night program. She loved the funny way these little ones looked at the world, and often got a kick out of things they said.

When speaking of Creation, one little girl explained, "God just took a lump of play dough and made man."

One of the cherubs upon hearing a leader praying, "Lord, You are Maker of heaven and earth, and we are but dust. . ." asked in a loud voice, "What's *butt dust?*"

Often in their innocence, they were painfully honest. One time Lorraine had fallen and broken a bone in her foot, and one of her little intercessors prayed, "Lord, please help sister Lorraine not be so clumsy."

Another girl, when her group leader asked her to take a paper to Lorraine, stood before Lorraine and her coteacher and shouted back,

"The old one or the large one?"

When Lorraine had to get her front teeth pulled, she worried about what these honest little girls would say. She felt self-conscious, and what made it worse, her health insurance didn't cover dentures; it would be some time before she could afford the partial.

The first day she taught her class with her front teeth glaringly missing, she waited for comments as the girls said their verses, listened to their story, and made their craft. At some point, while they were coloring, one little girl decided to call attention to the "elephant in the room."

"You have no front teeth," she said, as if Lorraine may have been unaware of the fact.

The rest of the girls nodded.

"Yes, I know," Lorraine said.

They were all quiet as they thought about this.

One girl finally spoke up, "I lost my baby teeth—now I'm getting human teeth."

Lorraine tried to hold back a laugh.

Another one said, "Sister Lorraine, now you're just like us."

They all looked up nodding and beaming their toothless grins at Lorraine. At first she felt embarrassed, being equalized with a bunch of six-year-olds, but then she realized they could relate to her and accepted her. Ah, those honest and loving little girls!

We all have felt the sting of rejection, whether it's because of beliefs, appearance, or social standing. And we've basked in the warmth of love and acceptance. Nothing feels better than when someone knows all about us and loves us anyway. Ephesians 1:6 says we are accepted in the beloved. God loves us as we are, and our faith in Christ opens the way for us to come into God's presence and His loving acceptance.

COMMUNICATION GAP

Darlene Franklin

If I speak in the tongues of men or of angels, but do not have love,
I am only a resounding gong or a clanging cymbal.
1 CORINTHIANS 13:1 NIV

Throughout the years I have taught every age from infants through adults, but my love has always been children. I have an affinity for working with toddlers, engaging them in a game of peek a boo, singing them songs, recognizing them as important individuals.

Of course one of the biggest hurdles to overcome in teaching very young children is their lack of language skills. Over the years, I have learned how to interpret some of what they say, especially when the words come from the mouth of a beloved child or grandchild.

But growing up in New England as my mother's one and only offspring did little to prepare me for a memorable encounter with a newly verbal young child. During college, I spent a summer in Mexico City as a short-term missionary. After nine weeks of immersion in the culture, living with a local family, and working with a local church, I had gained a degree of language fluency. For example, I found it easier to follow the subtitles for the newly released movie *The Sting* than to listen to American slang from the 1930s.

When the time came to return to the United States, I traveled by bus. We crept from Mexico City through Chihuahua and crossed the Rio Grande at Laredo into Texas. I was home, back in the United States of America. Across the aisle from me sat a charming little girl, dressed in colorful shorts and top, her hair kept away from her face in corn rows. She decided to make me her new best friend, and she told me the story of her trip.

The only problem: I didn't understand a word she said. Nothing in my New England upbringing had prepared me for a deep Texas accent as interpreted by a youngster. I thought, "Send me back to Mexico. At least there I understand what they're saying."

No, I wasn't teaching that girl, not formally, anyway. She came to mind though, when my Bible college sent me to teach Sunday school at a Spanish-speaking church in New York City. I faced a classroom full of Spanish-speaking preschoolers. Between the different accents (Puerto Rican and Cuban Spanish, not Mexican) and the young age of my students, I couldn't quite fill in the blanks in their conversation. When they ran into problems making the week's art project work, I couldn't find the words to explain it better. (I had chosen something too difficult for the age, but that's another story.) One girl burst into tears.

I did what came naturally; I took the girl in my arms. I let Christ's love flow through me and bypass the language barrier. Her sobs stopped, and I showed her how to finish the project—without words.

That day I learned a lesson I never forgot. A teacher's most important qualification comes from his or her love for the pupils. That love will cover a lot of inadequacies.

Anything else is a clanging cymbal. Or a deep Texas twang.

Not Another Apple: Patience

Tell me and I forget. Teach me and I remember.
Involve me and I learn.

BENJAMIN FRANKLIN

FEATHER GIRL

Jean Fischer

*Jesus replied, "The Scriptures say, 'You must worship
the Lord your God and serve only him.' "*
LUKE 4:8 NLT

Sophia is a bubbly, five-year-old package of energy. She enters the classroom dancing. She can't sit without squirming, and when I ask the class a question, her hand is the first one in the air.

"Ooo. Ooo. Mrs. Johnson, I know! I know!" She bounces in her seat until I call on her, and if I don't, she deflates like a balloon.

Flamboyant is a word I connect with Sophie. She wears flashy clothing in gaudy colors. I wonder, sometimes, if her mom cares about the odd combinations her daughter wears to school: a yellow and green polka-dot skirt paired with a pink striped sweater; red and white striped, *Where's Waldo?* pants coupled with a fluorescent orange T-shirt; and even, the day after her birthday, a flouncy, pink princess costume. But then, I know how willful Sophia can be. Most likely, she wears whatever she wants.

One day, Sophie arrived wearing *the sweater*. I can't imagine where her mom bought it, or what she was thinking. The white, long-sleeved cardigan was too big for Sophie's small frame. Someone had rolled the sleeves so they didn't flop down beyond her hands, and the sweater's bottom fell way below her thighs. Attached to its front and back was a faux vest made of feathers, big ones like you'd see on an ostrich or emu.

"What an interesting sweater, Sophie!" I commented.

"Thank you, Mrs. Johnson."

"Where did you find it?"

"In the closet."

I had the class sit on the floor near the writing easel, and we began a lesson about describing words. I displayed a bag of popcorn and wrote *popcorn* on the white, dry-erase board.

"Let's think of words that describe how popcorn looks," I said.

Several students called out:

"Yellow."

"Lumpy."

"Bumpy."

"Blow!"

That last one was a whisper. I didn't know who said it, or if I'd even heard it. Maybe my mind was playing tricks.

"How does popcorn taste?" I asked.

"Buttery!" Sophia exclaimed.

"Salty."

"Yummy."

"Blow it!"

Again, it was a whisper. I turned from the easel and saw Sophia sitting in front of Jack and Marvin who looked guilty.

"How does popcorn sound?" I continued.

By now, the class was giggling hysterically.

"Blow it!"

"Blow!"

I turned around just in time to see Marvin pluck a feather from Sophia's sweater and blow it high into the air. None of the students focused on my lesson anymore. Sophia's sweater was the center of attention.

Dwelling on worldly interruptions is like blowing feathers around in the air. Satan loves using distractions as a way to shift our thoughts away from Jesus. When you find distractions a problem, try meditating on these words: "Let your eyes look straight ahead; fix your gaze directly before you" (Proverbs 4:25 NIV). Look straight ahead toward the Lord, and watch the distractions melt away.

THE LONG WAY HOME

Jean Fischer

Lord, I know that people's lives are not their own;
it is not for them to direct their steps.
JEREMIAH 10:23 NIV

The assignment was an easy one. I gave each student a worksheet and a street map of our town, and then I asked the class to find a buddy to work with. After much scrambling of chairs, the buddy system was in place, and the class awaited my instructions. I split the pairs into *A*'s and *B*'s.

"I want the *A*'s to tell the *B*'s how to get from school to your house. *A*'s, you will look at your map and give directions to your buddy. Starting from school, tell your buddy which streets to take to get to your house. Use directions like 'turn left' and 'turn right.' *B*'s, I want you to write the directions down and draw a line on your map to show how to get from school to your buddy's house."

As the students worked, I walked around giving help as needed. Most students grasped the assignment easily, but one pair, Adam and Seth, seemed to have problems.

"Left or right?" I heard Seth ask, exasperated.

"Left, I think," Adam answered. "No. Wait. Right!"

Seth sighed. "This is hard."

I looked at his paper and saw a long list of street names and left and right turns. His map was almost worn through from all the erasing.

"What's the problem?" I asked.

Seth, a shy little boy, almost whispered, "This is too hard."

Thinking that the problem might be with Adam's instructions, I reminded Adam to start at school and give Seth good, clear directions. I helped him navigate the first few streets. Then I left the boys to continue their work.

Before long, I heard Seth say, "Turn around? Are you sure? Now we're going back where we just came from!"

"I *know*," Adam replied, "but that's what he does."

He? I wondered who "he" was.

By now, the rest of the class had finished the assignment, and I had given the pairs another task to do.

"Boys," I said. "Are you still having trouble?"

Seth was nearly in tears. "I can't do this!" he whined. "It's too hard."

The line on Seth's map wove through town in a labyrinth of left and right turns. It reached a dead end on Madison Road and then made a U-turn back in the direction from which it came.

"Adam," I said. "Why are you giving Seth such complicated directions?"

"Because," Adam replied, clearly annoyed with me. "It *is* complicated. I take the bus, and my house is last on the route!"

As Christians, we don't need to worry about finding our way home, because God promises to guide us. When life seems like a maze of unfamiliar streets, remember this pearl of wisdom from Proverbs: "In their hearts humans plan their course, but the LORD establishes their steps." (Proverbs 16:9 NIV).

GOING TO SEE THE RABBITS

Jean Fischer

The Lord will guide you always.
ISAIAH 58:11 NIV

It's a sad day when a student moves away. This year, three students left our first-grade class when their families moved out of state.

Melissa and her family went to South Dakota.

"Where is South Dakota?" I asked the class, pointing to our big map of the United States.

Melissa was the only one to raise her hand. Proudly, she marched up to the map and pointed to *North* Dakota.

"Are you sure?" I asked her. Then we had a short lesson on compass directions.

"And what can you tell us about South Dakota?"

"You have to wear a warm jacket, and the rocks there have faces," Melissa answered. Hooray! A Mount Rushmore teaching moment.

Tyler and his parents were moving to Washington DC. That was a hard location to find on the map, but we found it and marked it so we'd all know where Tyler went.

"Washington is a very interesting place," I told Tyler after we'd had a class discussion about the famous monuments there. "What's the first thing you want to see when you get to your new home?"

"My bedroom," he answered.

Jackson was the third student to leave. I had known in advance about the other two, but Jackson's announcement came as a surprise.

"I'm movin'," he told me one morning as he hung his jacket in the coatroom. "I'm goin' in two weeks."

Jackson wasn't always truthful, and this came just days after his best friend, Tyler, moved away. I decided he was telling a fib. "That's nice, Jackson," I said. "Please take your seat."

Later that morning, Jackson came to me and tugged on my arm. "Aren't we gonna find me on the map?" he asked.

I gave him a blank look.

"My new home!" he said. "Aren't we gonna find me?"

"Jackson," I said. "Are you *really* moving?"

"Yup."

"Where are you going?"

"To see the rabbits," he said.

"Oh Jackson." I sighed. "You're not moving."

"I am!" he insisted. Jackson was so angry with me for the rest of the day that I almost believed him, but going to see the rabbits made no sense to me at all.

The next morning, Jackson was the first one into the classroom. He held a note in his chubby fist, and he thrust it at me. "Read this!" he commanded. "I am *too* going to see the rabbits!"

Jackson watched me unfold the note and read: *Dear Mrs. Williamson, Friday, October 15th, will be Jackson's last day in class. We are moving to Cedar Rapids. . ."*

I hate to see my students leave, but I know that God goes with them. Psalm 48:14 (NIV) says, "For this God is our God for ever and ever; he will be our guide even to the end." This assures us that God is with us wherever we go, loving us and guiding us all along the way.

NOT EXACTLY AS IT APPEARS

Shelley R. Lee

Tune your ears to the world of Wisdom; set your heart on a life of Understanding. . . Searching for it like a prospector panning for gold, like an adventurer on a treasure hunt, believe me, before you know it Fear-of-God will be yours; you'll have come upon the Knowledge of God.
PROVERBS 2:2, 4–5 MSG

The senior high school students were asked to complete a "Graduation Diploma Information" sheet. The directions read, "Use this form to specify *EXACTLY* how you want your name to appear on your diploma. *It is extremely important that you fill this out neatly and correctly.*"

The facilitating teacher, a friend of mine, surveyed the room to check on the students' progress and answer any questions if needed. They were all working intently, many of them quickly turning in the completed form, so he went back to work at his desk.

After some time he noticed one student in the back of the room was taking an earthly eternity to complete the form. The teacher went to check on her and found that she was attempting to write using her own form of calligraphy. It was apparent that she was untrained in the art of calligraphy. When asked what she was doing she replied, "I'm not really a great writer. You'd think they'd have a good writer do these."

She thought that her *exact* writing would appear on the diploma, as in, scanned and reprinted on her official document on graduation day. No wonder she was thinking a graphic artist should be a part of this process!

The teacher who told this story enjoyed a hearty chuckle over the misunderstood instructions. The student simply didn't fully understand the instructions, and the result was comedic.

I laughed when I heard this story, a bit self-righteously, I must confess. But God quickly brought to mind how many times I've misunderstood something that I truly thought I had rightly understood. Sometimes I make a judgment too quickly.

For example, the other day my husband was late for a dinner event where I was waiting with a coworker. He called me, and his first words were, "So, I was lying down. . ." I immediately thought he fell asleep and was telling me he was going to be very late. I quickly became angry with him. I soon learned that what he was trying to tell me was that he was lying down under the car trying to find the hide-a-key so he could bring the car I would prefer to ride in with him—but it wasn't his usual car so he didn't know where either key was.

Understanding. . .it's worth pursuing.

BAD DAY

Renae Brumbaugh

*As for me, I call to God, and the Lord saves me. . .
I cry out in distress, and he hears my voice.*
PSALM 55:16–17 NIV

I leaned my head on the driver's side window and thought, *No. This cannot be happening to me.* There, locked inside my car, were my keys.

Now, if that had been the only thing that had gone wrong, I'd have been in good shape. But no, the keys-locked-in-the-car incident was just one link in a chain of events that made my day. . .rotten.

First, I awoke with a 102 fever. Normally, that wouldn't be a big deal. I have sick days. I could use a sick day, right?

Wrong. You see, this was an important test day. Our principal had made it clear that the only excuse for missing one of those test days was. . .well. . .death. And I wasn't dead.

But I felt like death warmed over, so I decided to take my chances. I called in sick, then e-mailed my principal a pitiful, please-forgive-me-and-please-don't-fire-me-and-I'm-so-sorry note.

He forgave me. "Just get better," he said.

What a nice man.

But I still had to take my kids to school. After all, they weren't sick. I woke them, fed them each a granola bar, and told them to get dressed. Do you feel sorry for me? I hope so. I feel entitled to a little pity.

After I dropped them off, I thought I'd stop by my classroom and make sure everything was ready for the sub. With my head down, I sneaked into the building. I felt like a stealth bomber. But remember, I had a 102 fever, so I wasn't thinking clearly. I wasn't very stealth.

I was spotted. Oh well, at least I looked terrible. No one could accuse me of faking my illness.

I got in and out as fast as my poor, fever-racked body would allow. (Still looking for pity here, in case you didn't notice.) Then I decided the only thing that would make me feel better was a giant Slurpee. I drove to the convenience store, paid for the drink, headed back to the car, and, well. . .you know the rest. No keys.

So I did what any mature, independent woman whose husband was out of town would do. I called my daddy. I know, I'm a big girl and shouldn't be calling Daddy to save me. But I was sick. And pitiful. Before long, I was rescued.

It's a good thing we have our Father to rescue us, isn't it? Any time, night or day, He's there. As a matter of fact, He's there even before we call. He's already rescued us, through His Son Jesus Christ, and He stands ready to rescue us from any situation in which we may find ourselves. Even if He chooses not to remove us from our troubles, He'll come when we call, and He'll stay with us through even the worst of days.

NO TALKING

Renae Brumbaugh

"Teach me, and I will be quiet; show me where I have been wrong."
JOB 6:24 NIV

Doctor, I can't—(cough!) talk," I rasped.

Duh. She could clearly tell I had laryngitis. Even I knew that.

"Breathe deeply for me," she said, as she placed the cold, round disc on my chest.

I obeyed, and was sent into the nastiest, most pitiful coughing fit you've ever heard. I sounded like an eighty-year-old man who had smoked for sixty of those years.

The doctor looked at me with that teacher look. "Hmm. . . ," she said.

"What is it, Doc?" I asked.

"You have a nasty case of bronchitis and laryngitis. I'm ordering you to complete vocal rest. Do you have any allergies?"

"No, I can't think of—"

"Shhh. No talking. Have you ever taken a codeine cough suppressant before?"

"No, not that I—"

"Shhh. I said no talking. Are you on any medications?"

I shook my head.

She handed me a prescription for some super-duper-high-powered antibiotics and a codeine cough suppressant, and I knew this was serious business.

"Thank—(cough!) you," I told her.

"Shhh! No talking."

Obviously, the woman didn't know me very well. She had no idea what she was asking. I'm a teacher, for goodness' sake. I talk for a living.

I wonder if that's how my students feel sometimes when I ask them to be quiet. I'll ask them questions and then get on them if they talk out of turn.

They have things they want to say. Important things, about their lives and their perspectives and their points of view, and I really should be a better listener to them.

Yet, if my students can't be quiet and listen, they won't learn the important things I need to teach them. It's only by closing our mouths and opening our ears that we can hear—and understand—important information.

God must feel frustrated with me sometimes. Though I'm really good at requiring silence and good listening skills from my students, I'm not so great at practicing good listening skills myself. I tend to talk and talk and talk to God, telling Him all the things that are important to me and asking Him for items on my never-ending wish list. And while He wants to hear my thoughts, He also needs me to shut my mouth and listen sometimes. I need to learn the art of conversation with God—where both talking and listening take place. Otherwise, how will I ever learn?

I suppose this little bout of laryngitis might just turn out to be a good thing after all. Perhaps I'll use this quiet time to really listen to my students and find out what's important in their lives. I'll certainly try to listen to my heavenly Father more. I'll try to be a good learner, a good listener, and take in all the wisdom He wants to give me. And hopefully, I'll continue to do that even after I can talk again.

Teaching Outside the Box: Dedication

I touch the future. I teach.

Christa McAuliffe

COPILOTS

Deborah Bates Cavitt

*"Honor your father and your mother, so that you may
live long in the land the Lord your God is giving you."*
EXODUS 20:12 NIV

There are a lot of advantages to having a father who is a teacher. Two of the best advantages are traveling and summer vacations. My family saw over thirty states, Canada, and Old Mexico.

Sitting in the passenger seat of our 1960 Chevy station wagon, looking at the scenery, I was Dad's copilot. After all, I was the night owl of the family. He and Mom used to tell me—when Dad was going to school to get his master's degree in the '50s—I would keep him company until the wee hours of the morning while he studied. When Dad stopped to take catnaps during our vacations, I was his lookout and alarm clock. His encouragement and belief in me distracted me from thinking about the darkness.

One of our many trips included seeing the Grand Canyon. On one particular trip, Dad handed me a map, saying, "Debbie, how far is it to Phoenix?"

"I don't know," I said as I tried to open the map without it flying out the open car window. Back then we had *455 air-conditioning*—4 windows down at 55 miles per hour.

"Do you know how to read a map?" Dad asked me quizzically.

"No, not really."

Dad proceeded to give me a brief lesson on map reading. Then I remembered a previous fifth-grade teacher, Mr. Cutler at Godsman Elementary in Denver, telling us that from the bottom of the thumb to the middle joint was about one inch.

"Dad, it's about two inches," I announced proudly as I folded the map just right.

"I don't want to know in inches. Look at the legend." He pointed to the legend without taking his eyes from the road.

"Okay, it's about two hundred miles."

When we finally arrived, it was exceptionally windy at the Grand Canyon. Although the view was spectacular, I didn't want to get too close to the edge. I was afraid I would fall down the steep, colorful, creviced canyons.

Dad taught me how to use his new camera that made slides. I took a picture of my family. Then it was my turn to stand close to the edge. I didn't think twice. Dad's encouragement and a slight "picture-taking" distraction worked.

Dad is in his seventies now, recovered from a broken hip and has diabetes. "Some-timers" cataracts and his sight are so bad that he can't drive anymore. This past summer, my parents, my husband Al, and I traveled back to Colorado, New Mexico, and west Texas. Many mornings, Dad would knock on our hotel door to see if his *Night Owl* was awake and ready to go.

"Dad, we bought you a large-print atlas to use on the trip. About how far is it to New Mexico?" I asked.

"You would get a book, being a school librarian for the past twenty-five years, wouldn't you, Deborah Kay? Let's see, it's about two inches." We all chuckled, and he gave me a wink.

WHAT IF I HAVE NO TALENT?

Anita Higman

Each of you should use whatever gift you have received to serve others.
1 PETER 4:10 NIV

It all started with the words, "Mom, what if I have no talent?" That was the question my daughter, Hillary, asked countless times in junior high as I drove her to school. And on those occasions I would answer, "No one is born without talent. God gives everyone on earth special talents. Perhaps you just don't know what all of them are yet. But you will!"

What was my daughter's response to this? She had doubt the size of a rhino—the extra-large variety. Hillary didn't question the fact that God had given *other* people talents, but she thought God had simply forgotten *her*. As if she were a Mr. Potato Head toy missing some of the parts.

In the midst of all this anxiety, my daughter met an amazing choir director whom I will fondly call *Mr. B.* He was, in fact, a teacher who fulfilled the scripture about serving others with his gifts, and he did it well. Miraculously, after Hillary joined the choir she felt for the first time that she fit in somewhere. She began to sing, and the sound that came out of her mouth must have surprised her. Mr. B. encouraged and challenged Hillary and all of his students to do their best. Choir was hard work, but Hillary admired what her teacher was trying to accomplish with their voices—living art. She was part of the music, and she loved it. She now had a song in her soul!

Hillary went on to take choir in high school, play the lead role in a large musical, sing in the college choir, and take up the guitar as well. With her talent for guitar and voice she has led worship at church and for retreats and events. Today, along with a major in English, she is studying music in college. Music is in Hillary's blood. It was there all along—she just needed a teacher to show her the way and give her the confidence that God knew what He was doing.

Hillary will have a lifelong love of music because of Mr. B.— because of his sincere dedication, because of the creative wonder he infused into his students, and because he taught his students that hard work wasn't really like that pink gooey medicine they had to take as kids, but it was a privilege and a joy!

Thanks to Mr. B. my daughter no longer asks, "What if I have no talent?" She just knows. Not with an arrogant lift of her chin, but with a heart full of faith that God didn't forget her after all.

Perhaps each of us needs that reminder from time to time—that God doesn't make anything that is throwaway. We are not makeshift Mr. Potato Head people! God is in control of all the parts of our lives, including our talents, and they are not only soul-satisfying when used, but they can serve others, and bring the Maker of those gifts pleasure and glory!

GOT THE GOODS

Janice Hanna

Then Jesus said to the crowds and to his disciples:
"The teachers of the law and the Pharisees sit in Moses' seat.
So you must be careful to do everything they tell you. But do not
do what they do, for they do not practice what they preach."
MATTHEW 23:1–3 NIV

As a teacher, you find out what you're made of every time you step into a classroom. You play to your strengths and do what you can to disguise (or improve upon) your weaknesses. Every now and again the kids put you on the spot to see what you're made of. They want to know if you practice what you preach. This happened to me in the middle of a drama class back in 2000. I'd just told my students we would be opening the class time with a warm-up. I'd place several ordinary household items in a box—a pencil, a cotton swab, a bar of soap, and so on. The students were instructed to reach into the box, pull out an item, and talk about it—without pause—for sixty seconds straight.

One of my students suggested I show them how it was done. Now, mind you, I'd been an actress as a teen, even performed a bit as a twenty-something. But as a forty-year-old? Did I still have it in me to pull off a scene? These kids were counting on my expertise. Did I still have the goods?

I drew in a deep breath and approached the stage. Reaching into the box, I came out with a kitchen scrub brush. An ordinary kitchen scrub brush. How in the world could I talk about this for sixty seconds straight? I swallowed hard and stared at it. Then, for whatever reason, my mind kicked into gear, and off I went, singing the praises of this scrub brush, and even growing very emotional, letting the tears flow, and I extolled its many virtues. By the end, I held it close to my heart, like it was the dearest thing in the world to me. I claimed—with voice trembling—that I couldn't live without it. (And truly, what woman can live without her scrub brush?)

My class was eerily silent as I finished. Then a round of applause sounded. I wiped the tears from my eyes, faced the kids with a shrug, and said, "Well, there you go."

They never questioned my acting ability again. And when I asked them to do something—as their teacher/director—they took my advice, knowing I had the goods.

What about you? Have you ever been put to the test? Put on the spot? What if there were some sort of sixty-second challenge where the Lord said, "Okay, up on the stage. Show me that you really are who you say you are." Would you pass the test? If you've just been pretending, chances are pretty good you'd flop. But if you were genuine in your walk with Him, you could pull it off, no problem.

Life presents us with several "got the goods" opportunities, doesn't it! Next time you're faced with one, let it remind you to be genuine. *Real.* And not just for the sake of those watching. A "real" relationship with the King of kings and Lord of lords will change us from the inside out. So grab that scrub brush! Let's practice what we preach!

LEARN YOUR LESSON WELL

Janice Hanna

Whatever you have learned or received or heard from me, or seen in me—
put it into practice. And the God of peace will be with you.
<small>PHILIPPIANS 4:9 NIV</small>

I made the decision to homeschool my daughters out of practicality. My youngest daughter was chronically ill and struggled with learning disabilities. My oldest didn't appear to be handling public school as well as I'd hoped. She struggled with peer pressure and other issues. Because our situation was unique, I had to think outside the box, particularly when it came to learning styles.

To be honest, I was probably one of those homeschool moms who drove her kids a little crazy. I turned everyday things into learning experiences. A trip to the park turned out to be a science lesson. A visit to a local restaurant became a mathematics adventure. A trip to the zoo turned into a biology lesson. An ice-skating lesson became PE.

My children, who were homeschooled most of their lives, grew to expect—and hopefully, even appreciate—this about me. Oh sure, they probably rolled their eyes a time or two—say, when a trip to a local cemetery turned out to be a history lesson, but that didn't stop me. I felt compelled to teach through life's many opportunities. And what better way than hands-on, in the everyday things of life?

Everywhere we went, the lessons continued. We traveled our city, our state, and our country in search of opportunities to learn. And they were found at every turn! I did my best to keep the sense of wonder sparkling in my own eyes, so that my girls would catch the vision and fall in love with learning. And why not? Wasn't this part of the adventure God had planned for us, to live with an ongoing sense of anticipation and joy?

The lessons continued as our family faced personal challenges and hardships. Though difficult, nothing—no pain, no illness—was wasted. In my mind, I saw each as an opportunity to discover more about God's plan for our lives. And trust me, I learned as much as the kids, every step of the way.

What about you? Have you made up your mind to be on a "forever" learning curve? Are you willing for the Lord to teach all that He has in mind for you, so that you can live a good and happy life? If so, then you're just where He wants you to be. You are an apt pupil.

If we're paying attention, we'll see that there are lessons to be learned from absolutely everything we experience. The question isn't whether or not God wants to teach us. . .the only question is whether we're paying attention. Learning our lessons, and learning them well is what He asks of us. Then passing on what we've learned to others comes naturally.

My children are all grown now, but I've got six grandchildren. And so the cycle begins all over again. Just a couple of days ago I took my four-year-old granddaughter to the store to buy a tricycle. . .not for her, but to be given away as a Christmas gift to a needy child.

Yep. The lessons go on and on.

PET PEEVES AND TEACHER'S MUGS

Michelle Medlock Adams

I always thank my God for you and for the gracious gifts he has given you.
1 CORINTHIANS 1:4 NLT

I have a friend who is a wonderful high school teacher, and she loves her job. However, she is often overwhelmed with the amount of work on her plate. I suppose every vocation has its share of pet peeves, but her number one irritation regarding teaching? Public perception. She was up very late one night grading papers and thought she'd take a quick break to check her e-mail. Awaiting her was a Facebook message, inquiring about her plans for the weekend. My friend quickly responded that she wouldn't be doing anything besides grading student essays. The Facebook friend then answered, "Boo-hoo. What are you complaining about? You get off work at 3:30 every day, and you get the whole summer off!"

Really? Well, that was news to my friend. Her workday has never ended at 3:30, and those summers off? They are getting shorter and shorter. My friend, being the good sport that she is, simply posted a funny blurb about eating bonbons with her feet propped up on her teacher's desk—day in and day out—until the 3 p.m. bell rings when she is whisked away by limo and taken to her luxurious home where she spends hours planning fun excursions for that long summer off. Anyone who thinks teaching is an easy vocation should spend a few days substitute teaching. I speak from experience!

I have another friend who has taught for twenty years in the public school system, and when I recently shared with her that my oldest daughter was planning to major in elementary education, she teasingly said, "Unless God has appeared to her in the flesh and told her that she is supposed to be a teacher, talk her out of it." My friend was joking, but there was a tinge of truth to her comment, because she has experienced the rigorous life of a teacher firsthand. Having so many wonderful friends who are teachers has made me keenly aware of the sacrifices they make every day. The rewards? Sure, they get wonderful presents for Christmas (Who couldn't use another teacher's mug, right?), but the day-to-day perks aren't as obvious as my friend's Facebook commenter might believe. Still, teachers keep teaching and giving and encouraging because it's not just a job to them, it's a calling.

As I look back on the teachers who truly made a difference in my life, I can't help but smile. I wasn't appreciative when I was a student in their classrooms. I was a kid, and it was cooler to complain about homework than offer gratitude, but today I am thanking God for them. And, I'm really wishing I had given them a gift card to their favorite store instead of another "You're an A+ Teacher" mug each Christmas. If you've answered the high call of teaching, we celebrate you today. I pray your teaching days are filled with wormless apples, supportive parents, and the grace to do all that is asked of you.

SNAKES ALIVE!

Connie L. Peters

*Each of you should use whatever gift you have received to serve others,
as faithful stewards of God's grace in its various forms.*

1 PETER 4:10 NIV

When Billy, beaming with pride, brought a shoe box with holes in the lid into Georgia's classroom, she wasn't surprised. Billy lived with his grandmother (due to tough circumstances) and often brought in various critters from her garden.

In Georgia's twenty-five years of teaching, she saw her fifth-grade students as little human beings, worthy of respect and deserving of opportunities to express themselves. She always encouraged Billy to share the things he found in nature. He had shown them tiny toads, a small brown lizard, and various bugs and spiders.

As Georgia eyed the box, she wondered what it would be this time. A bug? A bird? A frog? When Billy lifted the lid, Georgia saw movement and at first had trouble focusing on the many writhing creatures. Then she realized. Snakes! Baby ones. *Lots* of them. About six to eight inches long, brown with pale stripes along their bodies, pink flicking tongues, constantly moving.

She knew the average garter snake litter numbered twenty-five, the females would eventually reach up to thirty-six inches long, and they were not poisonous. But, until then, she hadn't realized how quickly baby snakes could escape. Many were out and halfway across the floor before she and the students realized what had happened.

Her orderly classroom transformed to a chaotic scene: girls shrieking and climbing on their chairs, boys taking opportunity to show their bravery or scare the girls, and Billy and his friends bumping into desks and tripping over their own feet as they chased the panicky critters slithering in all directions. Even Georgia shouted orders from atop her desk.

The snakes blended in with the floor and when they stayed still, Billy and his friends found them hard to detect. After nearly thirty minutes of scrambling and searching for escapees, the boys finally had all the babies back in the box.

Georgia planted her feet back on solid ground. "Well!" she said cheerily. "Thanks for sharing, Billy. Who knew baby snakes could travel that fast? Or hide so well?" She could tell by his grin that the fiasco didn't damper his spirits.

That evening, Billy's grandmother called. "Billy said you weren't upset that he let the snakes escape."

"No, not at all," Georgia reassured the elderly woman. "He didn't do it on purpose. And he was so proud to share them with the class. It was a science lesson that all of the children won't likely forget."

"Billy said it was his 'funnest' day ever!"

Georgia retold the story to Billy's grandmother. She knew the woman could use a good laugh and trusted God would use the whole thing to encourage Billy and his grandmother, making it all worthwhile.

God gives everyone gifts, talents, and interests in various forms to help and encourage each other, even though it may be in the form of something out of the ordinary, like garter snakes.

The Teacher as Student: Forgiveness

The best learning I had came from teaching.

CORRIE TEN BOOM

WHEN I SAY, "QUIET..."

Kathy Douglas

"Be still, and know that I am God."
PSALM 46:10 NIV

Sometimes a teacher's "tough guy" approach backfires.

Sherry glared at her class of fifth graders. That morning, her thirty-five students, who had been squeezed into a classroom built for twenty-five, were chatty and disruptive. She moved the three worst offenders further from each other and closer to her. Now all of six inches instead of nine inches separated the gigglers from each other. Their desks hugged Sherry's.

Her quick fix failed. She had barely restarted her instruction again when the whispers and giggles from the misbehaving trio subtly but persistently pushed the entire class toward chaos. Not one to be physically demonstrative unless at her limit, Sherry had reached that point. She punctuated each syllable with exaggerated motions and borderline bellowing.

"When I say, *quiet,*" she said, speaking through clenched teeth, "I mean *quiet* as in *no talk-ing!*" She emphasized *no talk-ing* by beating out each syllable on her desk with a ruler.

"And when I say, *quiet*," she continued, opening her desk drawer and throwing in the ruler, "I mean, *quiet!*"

With that, she slammed the desk drawer as hard as she could. Sherry expected a confirming bang to silence the disrupters. . .except her thumb hung over the edge of the desk, right in line with the slammed drawer.

No resonating bang bounced off the classroom walls. Just a muted *thunk* as the drawer connected with Sherry's unsuspecting thumb. Uncontrollable tears sprang to Sherry's eyes immediately. Not a whisper, giggle, or word came from anyone in the room. In the sudden silence, Sherry had her students' attention.

Someone has said God speaks loudest in whispers. If that's so, in the quiet we hear Him best. Elijah heard God in the silence of a cave. Alone, frightened, running for his life, he decided to call it quits.

"You may as well finish me off here and now, Lord," he whined. "I'm the only one You've got left" (a loose paraphrase of 1 Kings 19:4, 10).

God doesn't do what the prophet asks. He tells him to go outside and watch an ear-splitting show. Yet God isn't in the destructive wind, the rock shattering, the earthquake, or the conflagration.

"After the fire came a gentle whisper" (1 Kings 19:12 NIV). The ensuing quiet got Elijah's attention. In the silence he heard God's whispered words.

Sherry's classroom silence lasted all of five seconds. Then the three unruly students busted up laughing. Tears ran down their faces, too, but theirs was from uncontrollable laughter.

Neither Sherry nor the rest of the class could resist. Everyone dissolved in laughter. With tears of both pain and amusement, Sherry unceremoniously stuck her throbbing thumb in her mouth.

Like Elijah, Sherry's ego was taken down a notch with a dose of humility. And like Elijah, she survived to continue teaching. As for her rowdy students? They survived their short-circuited tongue lashing, too.

"Amazingly," she adds, "the class was quiet the rest of the day. But it took longer than that for my dented thumb to stop throbbing!"

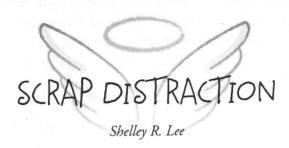

SCRAP DISTRACTION

Shelley R. Lee

So come on, let's leave the preschool fingerpainting exercises on
Christ and get on with the grand work of art. Grow up in Christ.
The basic foundational truths are in place: turning your back on
"salvation by self-help" and turning in trust toward God;
baptismal instructions; laying on of hands; resurrection of the dead;
eternal judgment. God helping us, we'll stay true to all that.
HEBREWS 6:1–3 MSG

I'm having trouble cutting out my turkey," said one little boy. He had
followed the outside edge line into the middle and cut the turkey
right in half.

"Okay, let's start again," I said, giving him a fresh turkey. "Let's
focus on the line."

His intent little face reflected the concentration it took to properly
cut out a whole turkey, and finally, only the directions that had been
printed outside the turkey edge line had fallen to the floor. According
to plan.

Another little boy ran up to me excitedly. "Can I have everybody's
directions that we cut off?"

I didn't see the harm in that; it was only trash. So I let him go around and ask the other students if he could have their trash clippings.

"Can I have these?" he asked with eager eyes. He grabbed the scraps and continued to work the room.

"You don't want those, do you?" he asked another student excitedly, now with a fistful of crumpled, odd-shaped, paper scraps.

He was having such fun with it. It was really cute, and it seemed a productive thing for him to do. He was cleaning up the mess and enjoying it, so it should all be fine. *I thought.* But something I noticed after cute began to wear off was that he was not working on his turkey project, which was the main objective of this pre-Thanksgiving class time. Very soon after this realization, I witnessed a subtle but distinct uprising in a little girl who apparently had become jealous of her classmate's joyous time. She began competing to get some of the scraps for herself. Soon one of her friends also caught the fever. Then it grew to a state of frenzy.

Now no one was working on the turkey project. They were either collecting scraps or distracted by those who were.

It was typical childlike behavior, I realized, but then I started thinking about how much it replicated what I call *adult behavior.* I get very busy with many activities that are productive and I may enjoy them a great deal. But often they are distractions from the main objective, my relationship with God, my faith.

God, help me not to be distracted by the scraps of life. Help me focus on what matters most.

HOPING HARD

Shelley R. Lee

We give thanks to God always for all of you, making mention of you in our prayers; constantly bearing in mind your work of faith and labor of love and steadfastness of hope in our Lord Jesus Christ in the presence of our God and Father.

1 THESSALONIANS 1:2–3 NASB

A good friend of mine asked his students to write about how they need to improve. The following is one student's assignment:

> *What I Need to Change*
> *What I think I need to change is my life. I have bad behavior some say, hang out with the wrong crowd, and don't prepair [sic] for the rest of my life. I'm not trying hard but I'm hoping hard. When really I need to work hard and hope hard in general. But more of the trying.*
>
> *I can change lightbulbs, batteries, holiday decks (decorations), water in fish tank, underwear, oil filter, oil, spark plugs, gas filter, toilet seat, locks on the door.*

I just love this student's sense of humor and his focus on what he can do. How often do we look so intently at what we are not yet doing quite so well, that we forget what we *can* do? And of course, laughing at ourselves is pretty healthy too! . . . Not to the point of forgetting what we should be working toward, but in a way that acknowledges where we are, so we can forgive ourselves and move on (because God already did).

This student's honesty is especially refreshing. I know, I've counted my hopes and prayers oftentimes, overlooking my efforts to work as hard as I should be on a particular thing.

I have many hopes and dreams, and I pray that God will give me the energy, favor, and steadfastness to get to them. When I pray about these things God reminds me that I must work in the effort, not just hope hard, as the young student also knew.

It is particularly encouraging that in the context of I Thessalonians 1, that it was their work for God—their labor of love—that was notable and remembered by the Thessalonians.

God, help us to be honest with ourselves, with healthy humor and forgiveness, that we would live today with hope as we work hard for You.

STARTING AT THE BEGINNING

Shelley R. Lee

*By this time you ought to be teachers yourselves, yet here I find you need
someone to sit down with you and go over the basics on God again,
starting from square one—baby's milk, when you should have been on solid
food long ago! Milk is for beginners, inexperienced in God's ways; solid food
is for the mature, who have some practice in telling right from wrong.*

HEBREWS 5:12–14 MSG

During quiet study time the fourth-grade class was working on a long math assignment packet.

Max came up to the desk with his hunk of stapled papers in hand. "I'm having trouble with this," he said, holding the packet up to my face as though I were hard of seeing.

"Really, what seems to be the problem?" I asked, holding back a mixture of indignation and laughter.

"See, I like to start at the end of the packet, the last page," he replied.

"Why is that?" I asked.

"I get the hardest page done first. Then I do the rest," he said.

I was surprised to find such logic in his answer. I looked at him quietly for a couple seconds and then explained, "Well Max, unfortunately for this assignment you have to start at the beginning in order to know how to do what is at the end."

"But I know how to do this kind of problem already."

"I believe you do, but the information you need to get the right answer can only be found by starting at the beginning and working your way through to the end. It's a complicated story problem," I said.

Max looked at me with disappointment and a bit of anger in his young eyes. He clearly wanted the quickest way to the end of that thick packet of math problems, and he certainly didn't lack knowledge in the subject.

It made me think of how often I want to do the very same thing. I think I have enough knowledge in an area of life. I don't think I need any further instruction, or experience for that matter, at this time. Yet God often brings me through things that seem very futile.

Why, God? I'm frequently wondering, even though I know He knows what He's doing.

And I think of zealous Max, eager to get to the end without fully engaging in the process of learning.

God, help me to be a teachable teacher.

WHAT THE STUDENT TAUGHT THE TEACHER

Roberta Tucker Brosius

Serve one another humbly in love. For the entire law is fulfilled in keeping this one command: "Love your neighbor as yourself."
GALATIANS 5:13–14 NIV

I didn't go to Jamaica to mop up an overflowing toilet in a rental cottage. My boss Bill, the school administrator, promised the mission trip would be a life-changing experience. . .not a Roto Rooter internship.

Fourteen high school seniors and their chaperones neared the end of our ten-day visit. We spent a grueling Wednesday before our flight home Thursday. In the morning we continued hauling stones down a narrow path to fill in the swampy ground around a church. A visit to an orphanage was scheduled for the afternoon, and a church service was planned for the evening.

Struggling with my heavy bucket of stones, I fought to resist the crabbiness simmering among the students in the morning heat. After lunch, I left the whiniest students at our two cottages with another chaperone.

The rest of us returned hours later—hot, sweaty, and emotionally drained—hoping for a shower before supper. Why was the line barely moving? I finally realized no one would enter one of the two bathrooms. After hemming and hawing, the kids who had stayed behind admitted a toilet had overflowed. They were waiting for a mommy to clean it up.

Slamming doors and muttering under my breath, I attempted to contain the flood. Thwarted by the locked mop closet, I threw towels on the indoor pond and stomped over to the other cottage for a disinfecting cleanser.

After finishing the disgusting job, I stood under the cool shower spray, my head pounding. I had lost my appetite for anything but two Tylenol.

Donning a robe, I lay on my bed to pout. "Mrs. Brosius," a timid voice called. "Are you coming to supper?"

"Not hungry. I'm going to nap," I replied in a rigidly polite voice. The cottage door closed. Unable to sleep, I dampened my pillowcase with tears. A few minutes later I heard a knock and, "Mrs. Brosius?"

Michelle and Ashley entered, carrying a tray laden with food. I sat up and wiped my nose, hoping my glasses would mask my red eyes. Michelle gave me a quick hug and left, but to my dismay, Ashley parked her body on the edge of my bed. She began to chatter about the Jamaicans, her boyfriend, school, and whatever else she thought would revive her wilted teacher, laughing periodically at her own jokes. I laughed, too, after noticing that our cook—knowing I despise canned peas—had hidden a solitary pea on my plate. When I couldn't eat another bite, Ashley hugged me and exited with the dirty dishes.

What a startling lesson I learned from my student! I thought I could stop serving when I grew tired of it or when the service required grew distasteful. Ashley had put in as hard a day as I had, but still found the energy and compassion to serve and encourage me.

My boss was right. Love is life changing. . .even when wading through toilet water to experience it.

PRANK NIGHT

Janice Hanna

*"Why do you look at the speck of sawdust in your brother's eye
and pay no attention to the plank in your own eye? How can you
say to your brother, 'Let me take the speck out of your eye,'
when all the time there is a plank in your own eye?"*

MATTHEW 7:3–4 NIV

As a theater teacher, I was used to watching my students pull pranks. What drama kid worth his weight in salt wouldn't pull a few good ones? But to do so in the middle of a show with a full audience looking on? That really took the cake.

My actors and actresses had taken the stage for their final performance of "Johnny Be Good," a musical comedy that had run all weekend. Their plan? To pull off approximately a dozen pranks on their fellow actors—and their directors—all in one final show. Seated in the audience, I was clueless. Until the first prank. Then the second. The third one went terribly awry, throwing everyone in the cast off. Suddenly, the script changed. Characters were speaking lines I've never heard before. These kids weren't winging it due to poor memorization skills. They'd actually rewritten the script. And, as the author of that script, I took personal offense.

You've never seen a chubby theater teacher run so fast in all of your life. By the time the kids ended the scene, I was backstage, ready to take them down. Unfortunately, I didn't even pause for a few breaths. I just lit right in—through clenched teeth I might add—telling them to never ever think about rewriting one of my scripts again. On and on I went with my passionate speech, giving them what for.

Only one problem. I forgot they were all wearing lav microphones. Oops.

Thankfully, with the orchestra playing, my passionate speech wasn't heard by the audience, (or so I was told). I settled back into my seat, doing my best to calm down and watch the rest of the first act in peace.

When we took a break for intermission, my codirector rose like a phoenix from the ashes of the orchestra pit, where she'd been playing keyboard. Unlike me, she hadn't had an opportunity to voice her frustration to the kids after the initial offense. I took one look at her bugged eyes, then followed her backstage, where she proceeded to have a "Come to Jesus" meeting with the cast. There wasn't a dry eye in the place. We knocked the fear of God into them, for sure.

Still, as I settled back into my seat for Act II, I couldn't help but think about something. How did God feel all of the many times I'd attempted to rewrite His script? Many times I'd added lines here, taken away lines there, all in an attempt to twist my life's scenes to my liking.

Maybe you can relate. Surely there are bits and pieces of your life script that are harder to take than others. And maybe, like my students, you've tried to rewrite the lines. Oh, how we need to learn to trust God! He created us, and He's got great plans for us. If only we can take our hands off!

These days, I'm not so quick to judge my students. Nope. I'm far too busy pulling the plank out of my own eye.

BANGLES AND BOLDNESS

Michelle Medlock Adams

Let us therefore come boldly unto the throne of grace,
that we may obtain mercy, and find grace to help in time of need.
HEBREWS 4:16 KJV

Math has never really been my thing. Yes, I was an A and B student throughout my education, but I had to study really hard to pull a B in Algebra II and Geometry, and let's not even talk about Calculus. Sheesh! So math was intimidating all by itself—throw in the most-feared math teacher, Captain Conner—and I was a neurotic mess. Picture this: It was my sophomore year in high school, and I was sitting in Captain Conner's Algebra II lecture hall along with forty or so classmates. We were furiously copying notes from his overhead teaching that day, and I was so into it that I didn't notice all eyes were on me. Apparently, my fashionable bangle bracelets were banging around and creating quite a disruption. As I looked up to copy that last formula, my eyes met Captain Conner's. I literally stopped breathing for a few seconds.

"Please remove your bracelets," he said in his stern "Captain Conner" voice.

"Yes sir," I muttered, clamoring to take off the bangles. Of course, I was so nervous that I inadvertently threw the bracelets off my wrist and across the room until they hit the wall and landed on the floor. I looked at the bracelets and then back at Mr. Conner, who had cracked a slight smile by now. I truly hoped the earth would open up and swallow me. It didn't. I somehow survived "the bangle incident" and even managed to pass Algebra II that semester, but I pretty much avoided him the rest of my high school career.

Years later when I was the education reporter for our local newspaper, I had to interview Mr. Conner who had been promoted to BNLHS principal. When I entered his office, fear gripped my heart as I thanked him for allowing me to question him. (By the way, I did not wear any bangle bracelets this time.) I expected to encounter "Captain Conner," but instead I found mild-mannered Mr. Conner, so nice and accommodating. He spoke highly of my husband and my writing accomplishments and even commented on what great students we had been in high school. As I left his office, I couldn't help but smile. It was at that moment I realized so many of us approach God the same way I had dealt with Mr. Conner. I was scared to engage in conversation with Mr. Conner because I was nervous he would remember the dreaded bangle incident, which he had long forgotten. In fact, Mr. Conner only remembered the best about me.

God is the same way. Even though we mess up, He forgives us and no longer remembers our mistakes. Instead, He focuses on our strengths and shows us mercy. So, if you've been avoiding talking to God because of your past mistakes, today is your day to go boldly into the throne room. It won't be nearly as scary as Captain Conner's Algebra II class—promise!

Testing, Testing: Discipline

Effective teaching may be the hardest job there is.

WILLIAM GLASSER

THE HARD LINE

Kathy Douglas

*"Do not make light of the Lord's discipline, and do not lose heart
when he rebukes you, because the Lord disciplines the one he loves,
and he chastens everyone he accepts as his son."*

Hebrews 12:5–6 NIV

Cocky. That one word sums up my husband, Mark, in high school.
He went to an all-boys vocational school and, without the diversion
of girls, he appointed himself the class clown. Even in grade school—
back before "whacks" were considered assault and battery—he enjoyed
getting the "board of education" applied to his "seat of knowledge." He
relished showing off in front of his peers. He would laugh as he got the
whacks, further aggravating the disciplining teacher.

When he reached junior high school age, he and his buddies were
rounded up by the police and taken to Toledo, Ohio's CSI: Child Study
Institute. Their crime? Pummeling a neighbor man with snowballs. In
the 1960s, such activity brought a stern and quick response from the
police.

For most parents back then, including Mark's mortified mother,
CSI was a place for juvenile delinquents. For Mark, the visit to CSI

spelled *p-a-r-t-y t-i-m-e*. He and his buddies all together for a sleepover? They had no qualms about any CSI stigma. They entertained each other all night!

By the time he entered high school, Mark had become adept at irritating most authority figures, especially teachers. He was an average student with below-average deportment. His focus remained fun.

On the first day of class in his senior year, he and his rowdy friends sat at their desks waiting for the teacher. They didn't know anything about this instructor.

Where could he be anyway?

The second bell rang and still no teacher. Two minutes passed. The bantering and goofing off started.

"Maybe this guy isn't going to show up!"

"Hey! Maybe you should teach the class, Mark!"

"I just might! I'm as smart as any teacher I've ever had."

After another minute, the snide remarks had escalated to loud guffaws, dares, and borderline mayhem. Suddenly, in walked the teacher.

BANG!

He slammed the door behind him. Scowling and stomping, he walked across the front of the room. He kicked the garbage can, sending it clattering across the floor. He threw his books and papers down on the desk, regarding each of them with a look of pure contempt. No one spoke, smiled, or moved.

"I don't want to be here!" he shouted. "I'm sure none of you *!#*!!#*s is any smarter than a *#*!!#*ing cockroach! But here we are and you're gonna learn if I have to kick your silly *#**s from here to Timbuktu!"

Even mouthy Mark was dumbstruck—paralyzed with fear.

Sometimes God takes a hard line with us, too. His rebuke and corrective discipline come from His holiness and love. He doesn't settle for anything less. He desires our best.

Mark chuckles whenever he tells his favorite teacher story. "You know what?" he says. "That teacher was the nicest guy. He never swore or raised his voice in class again. We didn't need another performance. He had us!"

Additionally, my husband says in retrospect, "We all really learned a lot from him, too. And we *never* acted up in his class."

HEART DISSECTION

Janice Hanna

Create in me a pure heart, O God, and renew a steadfast spirit within me. Do not cast me from your presence or take your Holy Spirit from me.
PSALM 51:10–11 NIV

As a student I was always extremely right brained. Give me the artsy approach any day. As a teacher, I used the same creative slant to teach my students, even when it came to the tough stuff: biology. Okay, so I have to admit, there's only so far you can go in being creative in a science classroom, but I gave it my best shot. And I knew my limits. When it came to, say, dissection, I decided to call on the experts. After all, I couldn't even butcher a chicken for frying. How would I ever lead my students through the process of a dissection if I couldn't handle it myself?

Enter my good friend Wayne, a surgical nurse at a famous heart hospital in Houston's medical center. I asked him to bring with him the one thing I'd decided I couldn't purchase on my own—pigs' hearts. Gross.

Now, imagine a tenth-grade classroom filled with all girls. Yep. All girls. Can you hear the squealing? Can you see the near-gagging? Can you hear the complaints? If so, then you've got a clear picture of what this was like. Only, add something else. Our school was housed at a church, and our "dissection laboratory" was the church's kitchen. And trust me, you just haven't lived until you've seen a dozen squirming females cutting up pigs' hearts in the same kitchen where you just catered a wedding the weekend before. Some images are stuck in the brain forever!

A few of the girls were tougher than others, naturally. And a couple even enjoyed the experience, slicing and dicing like pros. One felt like she was going to be sick, but managed to keep things under control. Another shivered and shook, tears spilling over as she made the necessary cuts. I oversaw the whole thing, trying to keep my cool, and praying the lesson would pass quickly. My friend Wayne— God bless him—kept on going, in spite of all the angst from the not-so-happy girls.

Years have come and gone, but I'm reminded of that experience every time I step into the church's kitchen. The Lord has used the event to remind me of something else, as well. He longs to do a little heart dissection on me from time to time. Oh, not in the church's kitchen, necessarily. And not the literal, physical kind—I hope! But He wants to open me up—to get to the root of things—to see me deal with the deep and hidden pains that I've tucked away in my heart where no one can see them.

I don't always enjoy the experience. No thanks. Like those girls, I'd rather just forget the whole thing. Turn a blind eye. Skip the lesson and turn the page in the textbook. But God has other ideas. He longs to see me healed from the past. Healthy. Strong. And He's willing to go the distance, to take me "deep" with Him, where He can do a thorough work of dissection.

Hopefully it won't take a real scalpel to accomplish this. In the meantime, I'm off to the kitchen for some one-on-one time with Him.

BREAK A LEG

Janice Hanna

*But my eyes are fixed on you, Sovereign Lord; in you I take refuge—
do not give me over to death. Keep me safe from the traps set by
evildoers, from the snares they have laid for me.*

<small>PSALM 141:8–9 NIV</small>

Theater teachers routinely use the expression, "Break a leg" at the beginning of every show. It's a theatrical idiom meaning, "Good luck." There are nearly a dozen explanations for this odd phrase, but I've never really ascribed to any of them, especially not since 2007, when the phrase took on a whole different meaning to me.

I'd worked in theater for years, teaching students of all ages, and having a blast every step of the way! And I'd maneuvered a variety of stages back to front, side to side, even the backstage areas. No problem. On this particular day, however, I found myself in a new facility, strangely unfamiliar with the layout.

We'd just gathered on the stage to begin our preproduction meeting when I realized we were short a few chairs. No problem. I sprinted down the steps toward the auditorium to grab a few. Somehow—I'm still not sure how—I missed the bottom step and went sprawling onto the floor below. When I hit, I realized I'd done some damage to my ankle. In fact, I'd never felt such pain.

I knew the moment I glanced down that the situation was far worse than I'd imagined. And so did one of my students, who rushed to my side. I would later learn that I'd suffered a catastrophic break in my right ankle (four broken bones), a sprain in my left ankle, and a sprained left wrist.

Ironically, my young student managed to hold it together, calling for help and even praying for me while we waited for the ambulance to arrive. Somehow—perhaps because of the shock—I found the whole thing rather funny. I started cracking jokes, even keeping the others in the room in stitches—pun intended—while we waited. I had no way of knowing the ordeal that was to come. Four ambulance rides. Four hospitals. Two surgeries. Metal plates and screws. One rehab center. Weeks in a wheelchair. Walking with a cane. What a mess. And all because I missed a step. I wasn't watching where I was going.

Oh, what a tough lesson to learn! There's so much going on in the world around us, and the Lord longs for us to slow down and focus on Him, not just for our own protection, but so we know how to pray for others. When we keep our eyes riveted on the Lord, He guides us every step of the way.

I've been back in that theater hundreds of times since my accident and have directed several shows there. (Hey, when you fall off a horse, you've got to get right back up and ride again, right?) Only, one thing has changed. Now I never allow my students to use the phrase, "Break a leg" before a show. No way! One thing is for sure: every time I go near those steps, I slow down and watch where I'm going. My eyes never leave the spot in front of me. I've learned to keep my focus on what's really important.

A SKUNK IN THE TRUNK

Janice Hanna

Purge me with hyssop, and I shall be clean; wash me,
and I shall be whiter than snow.
PSALM 51:7 NKJV

In 2001 I had the rare privilege of teaching a group of drama students whose sole purpose was to spread the Gospel through their drama. After performing at several local and national outreaches, our team was invited to go to Ensenada, Mexico, on a missions trip. I jumped on the chance, though it meant driving from Houston, Texas, all the way to Los Angeles to meet the missionary's family, then due south through the Baja peninsula. I knew it would be worth it, just to spread the beautiful aroma of God's love to people who might not otherwise know Him.

We left early in the evening, determined to drive through the first night. I led the way in our family's minivan. My daughter followed in our SUV. Both vehicles were loaded with teens and twenty-somethings, who sang along with the radio at the top of their lungs and basically had the time of their lives.

About six hours into our trip—just about the time the kids were finally dozing off—I noticed something scurrying across the middle of the highway. Something black and white. . .with a long tail. Before I realized it, I'd run over a skunk. Immediately, the scent permeated our vehicle. This, of course, woke up the kids in a hurry. They began to complain aloud. But what could I do? I felt sure we'd shake the odor, but that didn't happen. The groaning from the kids went on for hours. How could we ever shake this horrible scent? It seemed to be part of us.

We stopped at a church in El Paso to sleep a few hours, then went on to a carwash afterward, hoping to wash away all traces of the dead skunk from the bottom of the minivan. No such luck. We scrubbed and scrubbed, but there was no removing the odor. At this point, I had to wonder if we would ever get rid of it.

My poor students! They had to make that whole trip—from Texas to California to Mexico—with the pervasive odor of skunk—in the vehicle, in the luggage, in their clothes. And all because their teacher made an error in judgment. I hadn't seen what was right in front of me until it was too late.

Maybe you can relate. Have you ever made an error in judgment that had lasting, stinky effects? Maybe you made a fast decision and it turned out to be the wrong one. Perhaps you followed after something that looked appealing, only to find out it was not what it appeared to be. Maybe you followed after the crowd, only to find out they'd led you to a trash heap.

We've all been there. Thank goodness, we serve a God who washes us white as snow, removing all remnants of our past stain (and odor). He doesn't just take us back to our former cleanliness. No, He covers us with His righteousness, purifying us from the inside-out.

I have to laugh when I think about that poor dead skunk. He gave his life so that I could learn a very tough—and very stinky—lesson.

THANKS FOR FLUNKING ME

Connie L. Peters

*God disciplines us for our good, in order that we may share in his
holiness. No discipline seems pleasant at the time, but painful.
Later on, however, it produces a harvest of righteousness
and peace for those who have been trained by it.*

HEBREWS 12:10–11 NIV

When the phone rang, Nancy wondered who with such a mature
voice was addressing her by her surname. In twenty years of teaching school, some students faded into the background of her memory,
some stuck out. Red hair and freckles flashed in her mind. "Jennifer!"

Jennifer was one who stuck out with her quirky sense of humor.
She was like an innocent child in some ways, but was also so mature that
on debate team trips, Nancy entrusted her with extra responsibilities.

"Yes! You remembered!" Jennifer seemed delighted that Nancy
recognized her voice. Nancy had even surprised herself, since it had
been at least fifteen years since she had last heard it.

How well she remembered Jennifer, one of her most capable
students! Jennifer had what it took to go far, but Nancy had to flunk
her. Her student simply did not do the work.

Surely Jennifer wasn't calling after all these years because she was still upset about her grade! How Jennifer had wheedled, cajoled, and begged Nancy to give her opportunity for extra credit! She had always gotten her way with other teachers, but Nancy expected better things of Jennifer. She had held firm.

Now to Nancy's surprise, Jennifer said, "I called to thank you for flunking me."

"To thank me for flunking you?" Nancy said in disbelief.

Jennifer laughed. "I am a teacher now. And if you had passed me, I wouldn't have worked as hard as I did in college."

"Well, you're welcome," said Nancy, feeling a little odd. She had been thanked for a lot of things over the years, but never for a failing grade.

"And I appreciate all the things you did for us on the debate team. You didn't have to do that. You sacrificed a lot to drive us across the country. I'm also a parent now. I know you had to take time away from your own family to be with us."

"Yes," Nancy said. "Well, you're welcome."

"I'll never forget what you said," Jennifer continued. "You said, 'You deserve this grade, but I love you anyway.' "

Nancy smiled. Through all the ups and downs of teaching high school students, she had learned one thing well: love them anyway. And because she expected more from them than they believed possible for themselves, she had to do the tough things.

Like Nancy, God loves His children and expects the best from us. As our loving Father and Creator, He knows our potential better than we do. He wants us to choose His way because it is the best for us. And when we don't, He disciplines us, and loves us anyway. And though it may seem a little weird; we need to thank Him for the discipline.

HIGH AS A KITE

Darlene Franklin

Forgetting what is behind and straining toward what is ahead,
I press on toward the goal to win the prize for which
God has called me heavenward in Christ Jesus.

PHILIPPIANS 3:13–14 NIV

Nancy Bailey drove to school one March morning in Lawton, a bustling community located in southwestern Oklahoma. The day dawned clear and bright, with a wind blowing "just right" for the day's activities. Her calendar marked the day as the annual "kite flying" festival for her third-grade students, a tradition that led to serious competition.

Students either spent hours constructing kites at home or they bought them at the store. Both were acceptable. They won prizes in categories ranging from which kite flew the highest, fastest, or farthest—to those which didn't fly at all. Very few left without some kind of recognition.

The kites waited on the windowsill throughout the long morning hours of reading, math, and other boring subjects until at last after lunch they went outside, eager to catch the wind with their kites.

Soon twenty-plus children raced down the playground. Problems appeared. A kite without a tail wouldn't fly straight. Make the wooden frame too heavy, and it won't fly at all. Store-bought kites, made of lightweight balsa wood, tended to do best.

The promise of the morning skies provided perfect weather, ideal for the outdoor activity. Many did well. Some students needed half an hour to reel their kites back in.

But one kite rocketed to the sky and raced along with the wind. J.B. was an average student, no scientific genius, but he could fly a kite like a jet pilot. He had a store-bought kite, but perhaps he had tied additional string to the spindle. That kite flew so high that it avoided ordinary obstacles like tree limbs and power lines. He ran and let out string. Wind caught the kite and pushed it west. He ran and let out more string. Again, it pushed forward, and forward, until it became scarcely more than a speck in the distance.

The wind pushed and pulled the kite until Nancy could only glimpse it high above the bachelor officers' club at nearby Fort Sill—a mile away from the school. She let out a breath of relief that during daytime, the officers were working. Who knew how servicemen might respond to a kite in their airspace.

The wind tugged one last time and at last the string snapped. The kite disappeared into the stratosphere. Heartbroken, J.B. began to cry. He had lost his magnificent kite—and his chance to outshine his fellow students.

Nancy comforted J.B. "It's okay. You did better than anyone else, getting it up there, and you kept it up there a long time." He stopped sniffling, and accepted the lion's share of the day's prizes.

How many times are we like J.B.? We pursue a goal, soar high into the heavens—and then we crash to the ground, heartbroken. We grieve what might have been instead of rejoicing in what is.

Paul admonishes us to forget what is behind. When we do that, we can let our kites soar as God directs.

RUNNING IN CIRCLES

Renae Brumbaugh

*Trust in the Lord with all your heart and lean not on
your own understanding; in all your ways submit to him,
and he will make your paths straight.*

PROVERBS 3:5–6 NIV

There's a famous football hero living at our house.

Well, he's not famous yet, but he will be. He told me so. He's eight years old, and someday he wants to play professional football for the team with the coolest uniforms. He told me that, too.

If the whole football thing doesn't work out, he wants to be a drummer. I'm counting on the football gig to pan out. Something tells me it pays better.

Last week, my future football star attended football camp. Our school's teachers and coaches worked with kids of all ages, encouraging them and teaching them important life skills like how to tackle and how to run really fast. They also taught them the importance of teamwork, and the benefits of persistence and hard work.

One afternoon after camp, I overheard a conversation between my son and his older sister. It went something like this:

Him: We ran a whole mile in football camp today.
Her: Really? Did you run a mile straight?
Him: No. We ran in a circle.

I know how he feels. Sometimes, it seems like I'm running in circles. Sometimes, no matter how persistent I am and how much I sweat, it feels like I'm not getting anywhere. I just keep covering the same ground, over and over again.

Take the laundry, for example. Just yesterday, it was all clean, folded neatly, and put away. This morning, there's a big pile of it waiting to be washed. And even though I made sure my kitchen sink was shining and empty before I went to bed last night, the dishes are already starting to pile up again.

Going in circles, I tell you.

It's not just the housework, either. It seems that no matter how hard I try to develop patience, kindness, and gentleness in my life, I keep winding up right back at the same place. I lose my patience. I act selfishly.

But I'll just bet my son's teachers would tell him that, even though he's running in circles, he's developing muscle and building stamina. In spite of the fact that he's covering the same ground over and over, he's getting stronger.

Come to think of it, I'll bet God would tell me the same thing. As long as I keep doing what He tells me, I'm getting stronger. I'm building stamina. My patience, though it's not unending, does last longer than it once did. And though I can still be pretty selfish at times, I'm kinder and more thoughtful than I would be if I didn't stay close to my Coach and follow His directions.

Not only that, but as long as I keep running and don't give up, He actually straightens out that road. Before I know it, I will look up and realize I've covered a lot more ground than I realized.

God's Lesson Plans:
Obedience

I do not believe there is a problem in this country or the world today which could not be settled if approached through the teaching of the Sermon on the Mount.

HARRY S. TRUMAN

COLOR-CODING THE LIBRARY

Deborah Bates Cavitt

"For I know the plans I have for you," declares the Lord, "plans to prosper you and not to harm you, plans to give you hope and a future."
JEREMIAH 29:11 NIV

It was our third trip to east Texas. This time I would meet with the school board.

My husband drove each time. We took major highways, a few farm roads, and finally arrived for the evening meeting.

The first time we came to east Texas— one year before—we saw only the superintendent in his office. We had a great interview up to the point when I said I had an out-of-state teaching certificate. In all of my interviews, no one had pointed that out as a problem. Therefore, he couldn't hire me. Yet he took the time to find a community college close to where I lived near Dallas to take the course I needed to become a Texas certified teacher.

At the end of that school year, I called the superintendent and told him I was certified.

He was elated because the librarian before me had other plans for the next school year, so he asked me to please come back to interview with him. This time I was able to tour the school. The school had two libraries: one for the elementary and one for the junior high and high school. I would be a K-12 librarian with a full-time aide to help me in whichever library I wasn't in for the day. After that interview, he told me I had to meet with the board. That meant a third trip. Everything happens in threes in the Bible. I prayed hard and often the following week.

After the school board meeting I had a job, a signed contract, and a smile on my face.

My prayer was answered.

I enjoyed everything about being a librarian. In the elementary library, I could read stories as little ones wanted to clamber on my lap. We sang songs, checked out books, and had a few puppet plays.

In the secondary library, I enjoyed the research and working with teachers' curriculum planning. This was all pre-computer. Best of all, I had student library aides who were most helpful in shelving, processing, and mending books.

Then it was time for our state library conference. I was gone for three days in a row. The conference was exciting, and I learned many new study skills and saw the new books coming out for the following year.

At the time, my student aides stayed in their classes, my full-time aide stayed in the elementary library, and a substitute was hired who had never been in a school library.

I returned to school enthused and excited to share what I learned at the conference.

I unlocked the library doors and my mouth fell open. I laid everything in my arms on the first table nearest the door. I thought I was seeing things. I looked around the room again. This sub had taken every single book and put them on the shelves by the color of the book. All of the red books were together, all the blue books were together, and so on.

Fortunately, I had the world's greatest student aides. Each student claimed a section of the library. All of us proceeded to place the books on the tables by the Dewey Decimal System (nonfiction numbers) or fiction. Books were everywhere, but in order. Teachers sent more students to shelve the books. I had a great staff, and I appreciated the library aides all the more. By the end of the week, the eight of us were able to see results. The library was, once again, open for business.

DAD'S WISDOM AS A TEACHER

Deborah Bates Cavitt

Listen to advice and accept discipline,
and at the end you will be counted among the wise.
PROVERBS 19:20 NIV

Do dads really know best? My dad told me in eighth grade, "Debbie, you will major in English and minor in library sciences in college."

Where did he get such an idea? I read when I babysat. I read when I was grounded. My allowance always provided one more new book to join the others on the shelf in my closet. Maybe Dad came to that conclusion because my state test scores were high in vocabulary. Besides, he was a great math teacher and could decipher those tests better than I.

"Dad, how could you say that? Just because I wear glasses doesn't mean I'm going to say *shhhh* all my life. I fully intend to get married someday and have kids. I absolutely refuse to wear long gray skirts and those awful orthopedic shoes."

Before long, it was 1970. I attended a school that allowed me to be a senior in high school in the morning and a college freshman in the afternoon. Where did I work part-time? You guessed it. . .in the library.

That didn't steer me away from what I wanted to major in—drama. I auditioned for many plays, but never did a part come my way.

Our family moved to Indiana. I chose to major in social work. At that time, I wanted to help all the starving and needy kids in the Appalachian Mountains.

Along this journey, I started writing poetry for the college newspaper. War. Peace. Love. I discovered I loved to write. I signed up for a writing course. Dad hung up on the writing school. *Does he know best?* I wondered.

Reading social case histories was boring and usually left me in tears. Dad sat me down, said, "Debbie, you have to be out of school in a year. Your sister will be going to college, and I can't afford two young ladies in school at the same time. You need to change your major." After all, what was my work-study job? I worked in book-processing in the library.

I was grateful, though maybe not when I was young and didn't know teacher-dads guided you along life's pathways just like schoolteachers. My dad's words guided me:

"Debbie, use your drama by acting out the picture books. Use the social work by helping your students, no matter their home life. I know you'll take their problems home with you, too. Your love of reading will sparkle in the library."

For thirty years, I've been a librarian. I have incorporated all his words of encouragement. Yes, there are days that I wear a long gray jumper and my orthopedic shoes. I did marry, and we have two wonderful sons, a wonderful daughter-in-law, and the blessing of two grandsons. Yes, there were days I had to say, "*Shhhh*" before I retired.

Did my dad know best? Yes. After all, he retired after being in education over thirty years, too. Thanks, Teacher-dad for your wisdom, words, and support.

NAME GAME

Roberta Tucker Brosius

But the gatekeeper opens the gate for the shepherd,
and he goes in through it. The sheep know their shepherd's voice.
He calls each of them by name and leads them out.

JOHN 10:2–3 CEV

Little Grace seemed both delighted and confused to see me at her grandmother's church. Grace had never encountered me outside of the academy where she attended first grade and I taught high school. We greeted each other and chatted a few minutes, and continued to do so Sunday after Sunday.

After a few weeks, it dawned on Grace that she was the only one calling me Mrs. Brosius. Everyone else at church casually used my first name, Roberta, so she decided to give it a try. Her grandma and I quickly corrected her, but I could see she didn't understand why only she was denied the privilege of familiarity.

The next day at school, out of the line of elementary students, I heard Grace's voice calling out, "Hi, Roberta!" As the week continued, Grace received several reprimands and the warning of discipline if she persisted. I don't think she ever understood why she shouldn't use my first name, but she stopped. Instead, she began to call me Mrs. Wilt, another teacher's name!

My colleague Vicky, a third-grade teacher, had a similar situation years ago with her own son. Mikey was five years old and newly enrolled at the academy. He would attend "Miss Smith's" kindergarten class. The only problem was, Mikey had known Lisa Smith his whole life. He saw her at church at least once a week and called her "Lisa."

Vicky began coaching her son weeks in advance, "Miss Smith is Lisa's school name. At church you may call her Lisa, but at school you must call her Miss Smith." A bright little guy, Mikey seemed to get it.

The first day of school dawned, and Mikey arrived, decked out in a new outfit, carrying a new backpack full of new school supplies. It wasn't long before he encountered Miss Smith in the hallway.

"Mikey!" she greeted him with a big hug. "I'm so happy to see you!"

Mikey pulled away and solemnly replied, "Miss Smith, my school name is Michael."

We've all been called many different names throughout our lives. Our parents chose monikers with deep meaning and the proper syllable count to match the family name. When they saw how cute we actually were, they quickly abandoned them for titles like *Peanut*, *Princess*, or *Pumpkin*. (Of course, when they used the full birth certificate designation, we knew we were in trouble.) Later, our friends gave us nicknames, some of which we will never live down.

Later still, many of us—women, in particular—traded our birth family names for the family names of the men who won our hearts. We've also been pleased to wear the labels *Aunt* or *Uncle*, *Mom* or *Dad*, *Grandma* or *Grandpa*.

Whatever name a student or anyone else uses to get my attention doesn't matter in the long run. What matters is that when the Good Shepherd calls my name, I recognize His voice, and follow Him.

LET YOUR LIGHT SHINE

Michelle Medlock Adams

"In the same way, let your light shine before others,
that they may see your good deeds and glorify your Father in heaven."
MATTHEW 5:16 NIV

When my daughters were in elementary school, we had the same routine every morning. As they grabbed their backpacks and headed out the door for school, I would always say, "Let your lights shine for Jesus. You may be the only Jesus some people ever see."

Abby and Allyson would always smile and say in unison, "We know, Mom." Now that they are teenagers, I still remind them of that truth from time to time. They still give me that "cheesy grin" and occasionally roll their eyes as if to say, "Yeah, we got it, Mom," but that doesn't keep me from saying it. They may have grown tired of hearing it over the years, but my hope is that they never tire of living it. We don't have to wear "Jesus Saves" T-shirts or post "Got God?" bumper stickers on our SUVs in order to share the love of God. We can reach many hearts for Him simply by living out our faith in front of others on a daily basis.

Teachers in the public school system definitely have to let their

Christian lives do the talking due to restrictions on what can and can't be said in the classroom. It's becoming more restrictive every year, but that doesn't mean our lights can't shine brighter than ever before.

I know many Christian teachers who live out their faith in the public school system, and their godly examples touch many. They offer words of encouragement to students who only hear how stupid they are at home. They give smiles to every student—not just the ones who are dressed the nicest or smell the best. They find ways to show the love of God through little acts of kindness, and those little things make a big impact on all who encounter them. Those are the teachers who inspire me to be better, and those are the teachers who make wonderful role models for my girls. I am thankful for those teachers. In fact, I want to be more like them. I want the light of Jesus to shine so brightly in me that it warms all those around me. I hope you'll share with me in that goal and let your light shine for Jesus. Remember, you may be the only Jesus some people ever see.

ALL OR NOTHING

Darlene Franklin

Whatever you do, work at it with all your heart,
as working for the Lord, not for human masters.
COLOSSIANS 3:23 NIV

Third-grade student Darrell was like the song in the Rodgers &
Hammerstein musical *Oklahoma*. For him, it was all or nothing.
Not that the eight-year-old had ever heard the lyrics from the musical
that spawned Oklahoma's state song.

Darrell possessed that winning combination of intelligence and
athletic ability. He loved baseball and basketball. He played three
different positions in baseball—first base, catcher, and shortstop—well
enough to play on the all-star team at the county level. The speed of the
pitcher's ball at the all-star game surprised him the first time he faced
it, but he adjusted and excelled. In basketball, he easily made baskets
from anywhere on the court.

Since Darrell excelled at sports, his mother enrolled him in soccer.
But he didn't like soccer. Instead of showcasing his natural abilities, he
chose to fail. If a ball headed in his direction, he'd stand still and watch
it roll between his legs rather than kicking it forward.

Darrell approached math with the same enthusiasm he used to tackle baseball and basketball. He finished his assignments early and came to his teacher, Nancy Bailey, begging for more work. After school, she wrote problems on the board for him to solve. Nothing she tried stumped him. He even figured out the answer to *three-to-the-ninth power* (19,683), a sixth-grade exercise that might cause a lot of adults problems.

Darrell also was a good reading student, but he liked spelling about as much as he liked soccer. When time came for the annual spelling bee, he refused to buy one of the study booklets provided by the *Daily Oklahoman*. That became his excuse for avoiding the contest.

As co-coordinator of the spelling bee, Nancy studied every word on the list. The booklet only provided the words; she and her coworker had to research the parts of speech, meanings, pronunciations, as well as write sample sentences.

Frequently she asked Darrell, "Are you going to take part in the spelling bee?"

He always answered, "No, I don't want to. I don't have the book. "

The day before the contest, Nancy gave it a final shot. "Darrell, you really should take part in the spelling bee. You'll do well."

"Nope, I haven't studied."

"How do you spell 'magazine'?" The word was one of the hardest on the late fourth-grade level.

"M-a-g-a-z-i-n-e."

"That's right!"

But Darrell still refused to take part in the spelling bee.

The following afternoon, the winning student clinched victory—by spelling "magazine."

Darrell didn't regret not taking part in the spelling bee, but Nancy never forgot.

Like Darrell, we may be tempted to only put effort into something we enjoy doing. Giving God our all comes easily when we do something we enjoy as much as Darrell enjoyed math, baseball, and basketball.

But if God sends us to a spelling bee instead, He desires that we work with all our heart.

We don't get to pick and choose.

BEGINNING AT THE END

Renae Brumbaugh

Straining toward what is ahead, I press on toward the goal to win the prize for which God has called me heavenward in Christ Jesus.
<small>PHILIPPIANS 3:13–14 NIV</small>

As I recently sat in a teacher in-service, I was reminded of some keys to good teaching. One of the first things we were told to do when planning a lesson was, "Keep the end in mind."

In other words, what do I want my students to accomplish? What are the goals for the end of the period, the semester, and the year? Once I've determined the goal, I need to make sure everything in my lesson plans leads toward that end. Teachers who do this usually see a higher rate of student success.

I should really end this story right here and now. After all, I don't know who will read this, and I honestly don't want my principal or the superintendant or the school board president to know that, as I sat in teacher in-service, I did something else. So if any of those people are reading this, please disregard the remainder of this piece. The end. Thank you very much.

But for the rest of you, I must admit. My mind wandered. While

I was supposed to be paying attention, taking notes, and hanging on every word, I got stuck thinking about keeping the end in mind. At the end of my life, what do I want to have accomplished?

At this point, I'm not sure my goal of being a multibillionaire is feasible. At least, not unless teachers get a ginormous pay raise. Even then, when word gets out that my mind wandered during teacher in-service, my chances for that kind of raise are pretty much shot.

My goal of being a Pulitzer-prize-winning novelist is still a possibility. Not a probability, but still. A girl can hope.

When I get to the end of my life, I want my children to know they were loved more than life itself. I want my family to know they were more important to me than anything. I want the people around me to know I cared.

It's funny, though. I'm not sure all of my daily lesson plans are leading to that point. Perhaps I need to make some adjustments.

Maybe I need to turn off the television so my children will know that they're more important to me than HGTV. Maybe I need to take a few deep breaths and answer gently, instead of responding to my family with impatience. Maybe I need to spend more time focusing on things that matter to other people, instead of being so wrapped up in myself.

It's not always easy to make adjustments in our lesson plans. But if we want to see success, we need to keep the end in mind, even if it means tossing out all the old plans and starting over. I think, somehow, it will all be worth it in the end.

ICE CREAM ZOO

Gena Maselli

"If God cares so wonderfully for wildflowers that are here today and thrown into the fire tomorrow, he will certainly care for you."
MATTHEW 6:30 NLT

It was Homeschool Day at the zoo, a special day that gave study-at-home families a chance to enjoy all the richness of the park at a fraction of the cost. Eager for the day to begin, I packed everything a smart mom should include:

Camera? Check.

Sunscreen? Check.

Hand sanitizer? Check.

Husband for corralling small children? Double check.

The kids were excited. I was excited. We were set to enjoy a field trip of animal exploration and see wild beasts up close. The new reptile and amphibian exhibit was especially enticing. The flyers billed it as "living art." Surely there would be enough colorful frogs and snakes to capture my children's attention and enthrall them in God's creative handiwork.

After entering the park, we made our way to the World of

Primates. We watched the spider monkeys, laughed at the baboons, and wondered just how safe the open air pit/cages that held the animals really were.

"Mom, look! There's an ice-cream shop," my daughter exclaimed, looking up at a directional sign. "Can we get some?"

"Sure, sweet pea, after lunch."

"Yea! We can get ice cream!" she exclaimed to her little brother, who cheered in response.

Onward we meandered through the African exhibit. First, we visited the giraffes.

"Mom, can we get ice cream now?"

"After lunch," I said.

We passed the elephants.

"When is lunch?"

I answered and continued herding our group. The rhinos were next.

"Is the ice-cream shop around here?" she pressed.

"No, it's at the other end of the park."

"Let's go to the other end of the park," she offered.

"We are here to see the animals," I said firmly. "We can get ice cream any time."

In silence she trudged on, but ice cream was never far from her mind. When we finally reached the ice-cream shop, each child ordered a single-scoop cone. Our family sat down at a picnic table to enjoy our treats.

"What's been your favorite part?" I asked. "Lions? Tigers? Bears?"

"Ice cream!" both children chimed.

"We could have saved ourselves a lot of money and just skipped the zoo and gone to the ice-cream shop by our house," my husband cracked.

As much as our kids enjoyed seeing the animals, they couldn't truly appreciate the day because they were too concerned about something as simple as ice cream.

I do that, too, I thought, as I watched them gobbling their cones. I get so focused on little things that I forget all the blessings God has already given me. It's as though I'm walking through the most amazing park that God designed just for me, and I'm too caught up in the little things to notice.

That day, like many days, my children reminded me of a great truth: Keep my eyes up. Instead of focusing on the things around me, I need to focus on the things above. When I do, I see just how much the Lord truly cares and provides for me.

SOCCER...BROADWAY STYLE

Gena Maselli

You can make many plans, but the Lord's purpose will prevail.
PROVERBS 19:21 NLT

As a homeschool mom, I wear lots of hats—science buff, math teacher, events coordinator, and even cafeteria lady. I fill each day with activities to keep my children engaged and challenged. This year, I looked forward to adding PE teacher to the mix.

I signed up my six-year-old daughter in a Christian soccer league about five miles from our home and began practicing. Dribbling, passing, running drills—within days she seemed to grasp the basics of the game.

During team practice, I noticed that she showed more interest in chatting on the sidelines than actually running after the ball, but I figured she was just getting her bearings. *This is her first experience with a competitive sport,* I reasoned. *She isn't used to stealing balls and jostling elbows. Surely she'll come around.*

After each practice, I went home with a new list of skills to conquer. She seemed to improve, and I congratulated myself on that improvement.

Then came *The Game.* It started like any other game. Our family had gathered in anticipation of her athletic prowess, but soon I noticed my daughter was missing from the group. While the rest of her team ran to attack the ball, my daughter remained in the middle of the field.

She wasn't preparing for a defense. She wasn't even cheering for her team. No, she was *twirling. . .and singing. . .and throwing her arms out dramatically*. It was a Broadway production at midfield.

Her coaches called for her to rejoin the game. She happily complied and skipped down field. Of course, the production wasn't over.

She finally stopped in front of the other team's goal. Again, she began twirling. Suddenly, the ball flew toward her, ricocheted off her legs, and landed dead-center in front of the other team's goal. An opponent slammed it into the net for a point.

She played the rest of the game with this same butterfly quality, flitting here, flitting there, but never really landing anywhere.

Where have I gone wrong? I wondered. Was she too young for this? Were my husband and I too lenient with her lack of attention? Or was she simply six? Whatever the reason, my plans for her stellar sports skills fell flat.

So often, all of us have ideas of how things should happen—with our students, our work, our lives. . . . And while plans are good, God's plans are the only ones that are sure to succeed.

With my daughter, I soon realized my error. I had unrealistic expectations, and I needed to let go. We continued to practice, but I stopped focusing on what I thought needed to be fixed and appreciated the fact that she was enjoying the game.

The season ended without her making any goals or any grand plays, but she improved and made friends. Most of all, she ended the season joyfully, with a grand bow, looking forward to the next. It may not have been what I anticipated, but it was exactly what she needed.

TO GIVE OR NOT TO GIVE

Gena Maselli

The generous will themselves be blessed,
for they share their food with the poor.
PROVERBS 22:9 NIV

Fall was in the air. The crisp November wind had begun to blow. Thanksgiving decorations adorned more than one home's lawn, and I was sitting across from my "students," trying to instill a dose of civic responsibility.

"Thanksgiving is coming," I said, "and Daddy and I thought it would be a good idea to give money to families so they can have Thanksgiving dinner."

My six-year-old daughter and four-year-old son stared at me. "Why can't they go to a store and buy their own food?" my daughter asked.

"Yeah," agreed her brother.

"Well, they don't have enough money to buy food. They need our help." Even during the leanest times, my children had never gone hungry. There had always been healthy dinners on the table, plentiful snacks in the pantry, and enough peanut butter and jelly sandwiches to keep their fingers sticky.

"Do you think it's a good idea?" I asked. "Should we help some families over Thanksgiving?"

They considered my proposal for a moment and then threw out a hearty, "Yeah!"

"Great! But here's the thing. It's going to cost $1.67 per person, and Daddy and I thought it would be good if you each paid for one person with your money. Daddy and I will give so several people can eat, but we think you should also give money from your banks."

"From my *Cars* bank?" my son asked, trying to grasp the idea of breaking open his Disney bank for someone else.

My daughter watched me as she considered giving from her own precious stash. "Why can't we just give *your* money?" she asked.

"Well, we're going to give, but we think it's good for you to give, too. We'll count out $1.67 from each of your banks." The homeschooling mom in me delighted at the idea of combining a practical math lesson with the spiritual discipline of giving and helping those in need.

"No, I think we should just give your money," my daughter said cautiously.

"Yeah," my son said gravely. I had clearly crossed the line.

How often had I been in the same place, wondering if what I felt the Holy Spirit leading me to give was too much. Too much time. Too much money. Too much of a bother. And yet, I knew that if my children could grasp the simplicity of giving at an early age, they would be in a better place spiritually and financially. They would understand that their money, like everything in their lives, belonged to the Lord.

"Keep thinking about it," I said, trying to hide my smile. "I know it's a lot, but I think it would be a fun family project."

My children eventually came around. A week later, they

gathered their banks and, with my help, counted out $1.67 each. It was a beginning. We had begun the journey toward good financial stewardship and giving hearts, a truly priceless gift.

Contributors

MICHELLE MEDLOCK ADAMS is an award-winning writer, earning top honors from the Associated Press, the Society of Professional Journalists, and the Hoosier State Press Association. Author of forty-four books, Michelle has also written thousands of articles for newspapers, websites, and magazines since graduating with a journalism degree from Indiana University. www.michellemedlockadams.com

ROBERTA TUCKER BROSIUS teaches at Watsontown Christian Academy in Pennsylvania, where she recently added a Cults & World Religions course to the Bible curricula she has developed for high school students. She has been published in newspapers, magazines, *The Secret Place,* and Barbour Publishing's *365-Day Fun Bible Fact Book.*

RENAE BRUMBAUGH lives in Texas with her hunky pastor/husband, two noisy children, and two dogs. She's authored four books in Barbour's Camp Club Girls series, *Morning Coffee with James* (Chalice Press), and has contributed to several anthologies. Her humor column and articles have appeared in publications across the country.

DEBORAH BATES CAVITT and her husband have recently moved just across the alley from her parents in Duncanville, Texas. They sit on Dad's patio talking about books, students, and grandkids. Deborah has written several articles, book reviews, and lesson plans for a library journal, *Library Media Connection.* She has a poem published in memory of her grandfather. She also has a selection in a Chicken Soup healthy living–themed book and a selection in *Hello Future*, a graduation gift book.

KATHY DOUGLAS enjoys leading women's Bible studies at her church, spoiling her four grandsons, in-line skating—and (rarely) target shooting—when she's not laughing at her husband's antics or running scared from his newest idea. You can read her blog at www.katherine-kathy-douglas.blogspot.com or find a listing of all her books on her website, www.katherinedouglas.com.

JEAN FISCHER has been writing for children for nearly three decades and has served as an editor with Golden Books. She has written with Thomas Kinkade, John MacArthur, and "Adventures in Odyssey," and is one of the authors for Barbour's Camp Club Girls series. A nature lover, Jean lives in Racine, Wisconsin.

DARLENE FRANKLIN is an award-winning author and speaker who has taught Sunday school and day care off and on for forty years. She recently signed the contract for her sixteenth book. Visit Darlene's blogs at www.darlenefranklinwrites.blogspot.com and http://thebookdoctorbd .blogspot.com.

ANITA HIGMAN is an award-winning author and has twenty-six books published (several coauthored) for adults and children, and she has been honored as a Barnes & Noble "Author of the Month" for Houston. Anita has a BA degree, combining speech communication, psychology, and art. Her favorite things include exotic teas, movies, and all things Jane Austen. She would love for you to visit her site at www.anitahigman.com.

SHELLEY R. LEE is the author of *Before I Knew You*, and *Mat Madness*. She has written numerous magazine and newspaper articles, contributed to *Heavenly Humor for the Dog Lover's Soul*, and recently wrote and compiled *You're Sweet* (Barbour Publishing). She resides in northwest Ohio with her husband of twenty-five years, a teacher and wrestling coach, and their four sons. She posts humorous stories regularly at www.shelleyrlee.blogspot.com.

GENA MASELLI is a professional writer and homeschooling mother of three active children. When she's not busy wiping noses, bottoms, and crayon marks off her walls, she is learning all she can about homeschooling and education and sharing it on her website, www.HomeschoolPassion.com. Gena lives in Fort Worth, Texas.

CONNIE L. PETERS writes fiction, poetry, and creative nonfiction for adults and children. Her work has appeared in numerous publications. She contributes regularly to presidentialprayerteam.com. Connie and her husband have two grown children and live in southwest Colorado where they are caregivers. Connie likes to sing, travel, and play canasta.

JANICE HANNA THOMPSON is the author of over sixty books for the Christian market. She lives in the Houston area near her children and grandchildren. Her days are spent writing, teaching, and planting kisses on some of the sweetest cheeks in town.

Scripture Index

Old Testament

Exodus
20:12. 137

Deuteronomy
31:11–13. 18

1 Samuel
16:7. 96

Job
6:24. 131
12:8–10. 73
32:8. 71

Psalms
8:3–4. 61
34:17–19. 101
46:10. 153
51:7. 178
51:10–11. 174
55:16–17. 129
126:1–2. 79
141:8–9. 176

Proverbs

1:5. 92
2:2, 4–5. 127
3:5–6. 185
15:23. 106
17:22. . . . . 57, 66
19:20. 194
19:21. 209
22:9. 211
23:18–19. 16
31:26. 87

Isaiah

43:19. 41
58:11. 124

Jeremiah

10:23. 122
29:11. . . . . 81, 191

New Testament

Matthew

5:16...199
6:30...206
7:3–4..165
18:15...24
19:14..110
23:1–3...142

Mark

7:6–7...36
13:34–37..63
14:38...11

Luke

4:8..119

John

10:2–3...196

Acts

17:11...39

Romans

6:13..51
12:6–8..89
12:7–8..59

1 Corinthians
1:4. 146
5:8. 46
13:1. 114
15:52. 21

Galatians
5:13–14. 162

Ephesians
1:4–5. 108
1:6–7. 112
4:23–24. 49
5:2. 94

Philippians
3:13–14. . . . . .182, 204
4:9. 144

Colossians
3:23. 201
3:24–25. 75

1 Thessalonians
1:2–3. 158
5:11. 104
5:13–14. 77

Titus

2:7–8. 26

Hebrews

4:16. 167
5:12–14. 160
6:1–3. 156
12:5–6. 171
12:10–11. 180
12:28. 33

James

1:5. 13
2:15–17. 98
4:13–15. 43

1 Peter

4:10. . . . . .140, 148

1 John

4:10. 28

ALSO AVAILABLE
FROM BARBOUR PUBLISHING

Heavenly Humor for the Cat Lover's Soul
978-1-60260-992-1

Heavenly Humor for the Dog Lover's Soul
978-1-60260-859-7

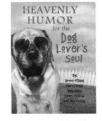

Heavenly Humor for the Woman's Soul
978-1-60260-030-0

Heavenly Humor for the Chocolate Lover's Soul
978-1-61626-245-7

Heavenly Humor for the Mother's Soul
978-1-61626-254-9